The Witches' Almanac

Spring 201.

CONTAINING pictorial and explicit delineations of the
magical phases of the Moon together with information about astrological
portents of the year to come and various aspects of occult knowledge
enabling all who read to improve their lives in the old manner.

The Witches' Almanac, Ltd.

Publishers   Providence, Rhode Island
www.TheWitchesAlmanac.com

Address all inquiries and information to
THE WITCHES' ALMANAC, LTD.
P.O. Box 1292
Newport, RI   02840-9998

10-ISBN: 1-881098-15-X
13-ISBN: 978-1-881098-15-7

ISSN: 1522-3183

First Printing June 2014

Printed in USA

Printed on recycled paper

Established 1971 by Elizabeth Pepper

Preface

THERE ARE TIMES when we feel challenged by our environment. Our physical bodies, our emotions, and even our faith can be tested. The very process of life is a trial — a soup of experiences, lessons, encounters, emotions, experiments, loves, and fears. Yet Karma lays the path for us and we walk the path attempting to evolve to a point where we can escape Samsara — the cycle of birth, life, death, and rebirth.

As often is the case, we find a difference in how the witch or magician looks at this mystery. We, as people in tune with nature, know that the obstacles will be placed in our way. We work to make each moment and each lifetime a productive one, knowing that we will return to experience the benefits of our past life's toil in the next life.

We strive to move ahead, pulling with us the race as a whole, into realms that are yet unseen and to experience energies yet untapped. Traveling this path, our very being becomes challenged. Although our physical and emotional selves are tested, many of us can endure this trial. It is when our faith becomes tested that we might crumble from the inside out.

Still, we can take control of our own destiny if we develop a symbol that defines stability to us and that is kept in the vault of our soul. This might be a love for another spirit, a star of Light, the words of a mentor, the awesomeness of deep space, the sun shining on our face, or any other "truth" that we know to be eternal. This forms the home of our strength, the power by which our faith remains and at times, becomes rejuvenated.

As always, with this understanding, extend the hand of love to your fellow creatures, and guide others to overcome misfortune and suffering. Spread the Light.

∞ HOLIDAYS ∞

Spring 2015 to Spring 2016

March 20 . . . . Vernal Equinox
April 1 . . . . All Fools' Day
April 30 . . . . Walpurgis Night
May 1 . . . . Beltane
May 8 . . . . White Lotus Day
May 9, 11, 13 . . . . Lemuria
May 29 . . . . Oak Apple Day
June 1 . . . . Vesak Day
June 5 . . . . Night of the Watchers
June 21 . . . . Summer Solstice
June 24 . . . . Midsummer
July 23 . . . . Ancient Egyptian New Year
July 31 . . . . Lughnassad Eve
August 1 . . . . Lammas
August 13 . . . . Diana's Day
August 17 . . . . Black Cat Appreciation Day
September 17 . . . . Ganesh Festival
September 22 . . . . Autumnal Equinox
October 31 . . . . Samhain Eve
November 1 . . . . Hallowmas
November 16 . . . . Hecate Night
December 17 . . . . Saturnalia
December 21 . . . . Winter Solstice
January 9 . . . . Feast of Janus
February 1 . . . . Oimelc Eve
February 2 . . . . Candlemas
February 15 . . . . Lupercalia
March 1 . . . . Matronalia
March 19 . . . . Minerva's Day

Art Director . . . . Karen Marks

Astrologer . . . . Dikki-Jo Mullen

Climatologist . . . . Tom C. Lang

Cover Art and Design . . . . Kathryn Sky-Peck

Production Consultant . . . . S. Perry

Sales . . . . Ellen Lynch

Shipping, Bookkeeping . . . . . D. Lamoureux

ANDREW THEITIC
Executive Editor

GREG ESPOSITO
Managing Editor

JEAN MARIE WALSH
Associate Editor

JUDIKA ILLES
Copy Editor

❧ CONTENTS ❧

CONTENTS

The Song of the Witches
Round the Walnut Tree of Beneventum

Hail to thee,
Weird walnut tree!

We are come, we are come,
we are come from afar,

By the glancing light
of the shooting star;

Some from the south,
and some from the north,

From the east, and the west,
we are all come forth,

Some o'er the land,
and some o'er the sea,

To hold our Sabbath
'neath the weird walnut-tree,

That tree of the awful
and mystic spell,

Where we dance the
roundels we love so well.

The gentle witch of Capua,
who comes of a gentle kind,

Hath floated softly hither on the
wings of the western wind;

The gentle witch, whose witcheries
the Capuan youth beguile,

With her arching brows,

and her cherry lips, and her
ever-changing smile;

But, though beauteous, and fair,
and gentle she be,

She must come and bend
to the weird walnut-tree.

And Medea is here from
her Colchian home,

A dragon she rides through
the white sea-foam.

Look at her eye with its
cold blue glare;

As lief rouse a
lioness from her lair.

But, though murd'ress and
fratricide she may be,

She must come and bend
to the weird walnut-tree.

And who is the seer
with the locks so white,

The wrinkled brow, and the
eye so bright?

His tottering limbs have
been hither borne

By a magic staff of the
wild blackthorn,

And from Vetulonia's
balls wends he,

To come and bend to the
weird walnut-tree.

Perimeda is here,
with the golden hair,

Beauteous, and blooming,
and buoyant and fair;

She has come in a car
drawn by peacocks three,

To bend at the shrine
of the weird walnut-tree.

And the fairy Calypso
has sped from her home;

She has left her grotto
and hyacinth flowers,

Her fruit tress, and birds
that sing all the day long,

Her gardens, and
violet-scented bowers;

In a nautilus-shell,
so pearly and clear,

She has sailed from her
isle in the Grecian Sea,

To join in our mystic
roundels here,

And bend to the wondrous
walnut-tree.

Hecate, hail! Hecate, hail!

Far has thou travell'd
o'er hill and dale;

By the dead man's tomb
thou hast stopped to alight,

Where the Lemures gibber
the livelong night,

And the ghoules eat the corpse
by the wan moonlight,

For such are the scenes
where thou takest delight.

Hail to thee, Hecate;
hail to thee thrice!

The Queen of Hades'
realm is here,

Bow to her, wizard,
and witch, and seer!

But, though the
Queen of Hades she be,

She must come and bend
to the weird walnut-tree.

And Gerda has hurried from
far Iceland,

She of the ruthless and
red right-hand;

A kraken has carried her
oe'r the sea,

To come and bend to the
weird walnut-tree.

We are come, we are come,
we are come from afar,

By the glancing light of the
shooting star;

Some from the south,
and some from the north,

From the east and the west
we are all come forth;

Some oe'r land, and
some oe'r sea,

To hold our Sabbath 'neath
the weird walnut tree.

Then a song to the tree,
the weird walnut-tree;

The king and the
chief of trees is he;

For, though ragged, and gnarl'd
and wither'd, and bare,

We bow the knee, and we
offer the prayer

To the weird walnut-tree
on the mystic night.

When we hold our Sabbath
'neath the pale moonlight.

Hail to Taburnus,
that mount of power,

And to Sabatus' stream
in this witching hour!

And hail to the serpent who
twines round the tree,

Whose age is known
but to wizards three,

Who was brought from the
land of ice and snow

By Saturn, in ages,
long, long ago.

And who sucks the blood
of one our band

Whene'er 'neath the tree
we take our stand.

Hail to them each,
and hail to them all!

Ho! Come with a whoop,
and a shout, and a call!

Join hand n hand,
and foot it full free,

Let us bound and dance
round the walnut-tree.

Elelen! Elelen! Evoe! Evoe!

For the witches who leap
round the weird walnut-tree.

– C.H.I.
Bentley's Miscellany , 1845

Yesterday, Today and Tomorrow
by Timi Chasen

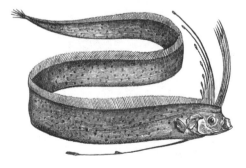

RISING OVER RUINS. Nobel laureate Derek Walcott declares, "The sigh of History rises over ruins, not landscapes…" suggesting that what is new is simply the past reconfigured. Though he was speaking on a figurative level in regards to the construction of poetry, the aphorism was recently borne out on a literal level in metropolitan Miami. Developers hoping to construct a luxury hotel and entertainment complex were expecting a routine excavation. Perhaps they'd find a few relics from the Royal Palm Hotel which occupied the site prior to its demolition in 1930 or perhaps even remnants of the Tequesta Indian burial mound that was demolished to make way for the Royal Palm in 1890. But as archaeologists dug past expected artifacts such as skeleton keys and antique bricks, they were stunned to encounter not mere fragments of Tequesta culture, but evidence of at least eight permanent structures that combined may have housed thousands of people at its peak.

These structures constitute the earliest example of urban planning yet uncovered in eastern North America. Though the site presents a unique glimpse into America's prehistoric past, progress marches forward. As of this writing, construction at the site has been postponed while the interests of developers and preservationists are mediated. One proffered compromise involves incorporating the excavated Tequesta foundations into an on-site museum, allowing once again the sigh of History to rise over (or rather with) ruins.

OARFISH AND OMENS

This year, Californians were treated to a rare and rather spooky sight: not one, but two giant oarfish washed up on California beaches in the space of a week. These massive silver-hued fish average ten feet long and sport a distinctive red dorsal fin running the entire

length of its body, ending in a fabulous red crest atop its head. Though common in temperate regions of the ocean, oarfish are seldom seen, so a beached one can be a frightening spectacle. Indeed, oarfish have ominous connotations in mythology. It is believed that giant oarfish are the basis for legends of sea serpents. In Japanese lore, oarfish are known as *Wani* and act as messengers of Watatsumi, Dragon Ruler of the Ocean. *Wani* were said to beach themselves as a warning of an impending cataclysm, usually a natural disaster such as an earthquake – not the best news for West Coast residents already living in fear of The Big One!

THE VOYNICH MANUSCRIPT. Discovered in an Italian monastery just over one hundred years ago, the Voynich manuscript has been confounding historians, cryptographers, and linguists alike ever since. The mysterious book, containing hundreds of illustrations of plants and volumes of script written in an unidentified language, has been the subject of intense scientific scrutiny and rampant amateur speculation, yet remains as inscrutable today as when it was first uncovered. Carbon dating confirms the vellum used in the manuscript was prepared sometime in the early 1400s; beyond that, nothing is known with any certainty. The book itself may have been written well after the vellum was prepared, so the historical origins of its content remain murky. Though the manuscript appears to be a botanical grimoire designed to consolidate and pass along valuable observations, it could really be anything. The indecipherable script could be nothing more than artistic gibberish;

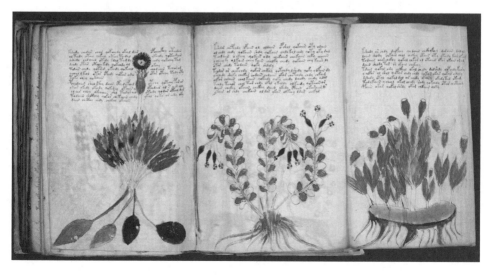

however, the seemingly random symbols, when subjected to scrutiny, appear to mimic the patterns of natural language. Theories on the manuscript's origins have ranged from the cynical (the book is a hoax) to the spectacular (the book is an ancient alien transmission). One recent attempt to decode the Voynich manuscript focuses on analysis of the botanical illustrations, rather than the seemingly alien script. Many of the plants depicted in the Voynich manuscript bear a striking resemblance to illustrations of Mexican botanica found in records dating from the mid-1500s. This new avenue of investigation suggests a North American rather than European origin. Skeptics are quick to note, however, that this revelation doesn't necessarily rule out a hoax…or aliens for that matter.

SPACE RATS, JELLY DOUGHNUTS, & OTHER MARS ANOMALIES. Humans have a knack for identifying patterns. While that trait has allowed us to grasp mathematics, chart planetary orbits, and win card games, it has also led to the peculiar phenomenon of apophenia or the tendency to see patterns where none exist. Apophenia can result in finding erroneous trends in statistical data or the face of God in a piece of toast. The search for life on Mars has provoked this phenomenon since the days of Earth-bound telescopes, when optical illusions were mistaken

1893 ad from a Chicago newspaper for "Kirk's Soap". It plays on the opening that year of the Yerkes Observatory's 1-meter (40-inch) refracting telescope (the largest of its type in the world), and the idea that Mars was populated with intelligent life.

for irrigation canals. As technology and space exploration advance, some apophenia-inspired delusions are exposed, but others inevitably take their place. Even high resolution pictures from the surface of Mars, beamed to Earth courtesy of Curiosity, NASA's latest rover, appear to show everything from giant rats to discarded jelly doughnuts – at least according to the amateur internet sleuths scouring the images for signs of extraterrestrial life. NASA is hopeful it will find some evidence of past or current life on Mars, but the evidence, if ever collected, will most likely not come in the form of rodents or pastries.

ABOMINABLE FORBEAR. Though the existence of critters on the surface of Mars has yet to be confirmed, crypto-zoologists nonetheless have something to celebrate. First, a brand new species of mammal, considered the holy grail of the discipline, was found hiding in plain sight: the olinguito, smallest member of the raccoon family, has been around for decades, but was mistaken for its more substantial cousin, the olingo. The discovery of a new mammal is extremely rare; rarer still is the resurrection of previously extinct animals. Purported Yeti hair samples found across the Himalayan region were analyzed for DNA and cross-referenced against a data bank of known species. The hair samples turned out to be a perfect match for an ancient species of polar bear thought to have been extinct (the genetic material against which the hair samples were compared came from a fossilized jaw bone, rather than a living specimen). This would seem to support certain Tibetan accounts of encounters with Yeti, which refer to the creature as a bear, rather than a primate. If true, this discovery could yield hope for the search for the thought-to-be extinct Tasmanian Tiger, already buoyed by credible witness accounts and undying optimism.

SLIP THE SURLY BONDS. The Voyager 1 space probe, launched in 1977, has officially entered interstellar space – that is, it has finally left our solar system and is now floating in the space between stars. The Voyager has now traveled farther than any man-made object in history. This is of particular significance because the Voyager is not just a piece of scientific equipment (although it continues to relay important information), but is also a sort of inanimate ambassador for the human race. Attached to the probe is a gold plated copper disc inscribed with information meant to tell Earth's story to any intelligent life that may happen across the artifact. The disc contains recording of greetings in over fifty languages, snippets of cross cultural musical compositions, and sounds meant to capture the natural world, such as chirping birds. It is also decorated in images, which convey the probe's origins in the universe. Now that Voyager has slipped the surly bonds of our solar system, the chances of it being encountered by another intelligent life form have increased. Let's hope they have a phonograph!

Dragon's Blood

DRAGON'S BLOOD or, in Latin, *Dracaena draco* is a tree resin that is reputed to contain the blood of elephants and dragons. Dracaena trees have a distinctive shape; a large base, then a pulled together middle. In the upper reaches of the tree, the branches spread out again to form an umbrella-shaped top. The plant is struggling in its native habitat and is an endangered species.

Dracaena is one of the oldest living trees on Earth and was a sacred tree of the Guanches of Tenerife in the Canaries, who once used it to embalm dead bodies. Dracaena resin is used as medicine, as varnish, incense, as a dye, and in alchemy and magic. Dragon's blood is said to quicken spells and add potency to any working.

Practical and medicinal uses
Dracaena terminalis is the variety used in China to make red lacquer. The roots can be made into a sugary syrup and also an intoxicating drink. This variety has been used to treat fevers and diarrhea. *Croton draco* is the Mexican variety (*Sangre del Drago*) that has been used as a wound herb. The ancient Romans, Greeks, and Arabs used *Dracaena cinnabari* (in English: cinnabar) as a dye and in paints, and as a remedy for lung and gastrointestinal problems, for wound healing, diarrhea, and skin problems, such as eczema.

According to Maude Grieve in her book *A Modern Herbal*, the resin was once used to treat syphilis. Dragon's blood has also been used for internal injuries such as trauma, postpartum bleeding, and menstrual problems.

Dragon's Blood Mojo Bags
In African-American Hoodoo and New Orleans Voodoo, the herb is used to make a trick bag, gris-gris, wanga, nation-sack, mojo-hand, or root-bag to attract luck, money, or love. To make the bag, use appropriately colored flannel cloth, such as red for a love mojo, green for a money mojo, white for a

baby blessing, light blue for a home blessing or for spiritual peace, or orange to incite change. Mojo bags may also be made of leather or cotton cloth.

The bag should contain at least three symbols representing your need, such as a petition paper with your wish written upon it (written in Dragon's blood ink for greatest effect), a seal or sigil (best drawn with Dragon's blood ink), coins, crystals, stones, herbs, and roots. The total number of ingredients should equal an odd number: 3, 5, 7, 9, 11, or 13. Add Dragon's blood resin to strengthen your bag.

After it is made, you must "fix" your bag. Smoke it with incense or in the smoke of a candle, or breathe on it to bring it to life. Make a petition to your patron god or goddess for aid, then tie, wrap, or sew the bag shut. This step is called "tying the mojo" and most practitioners use a miller's knot for this purpose.

Now "feed" your bag by sprinkling it with alcohol such as whisky (the "Waters of Life"), Florida water, or perfume (use your own bodily fluids for a sex magic bag). A tiny dab will do. You must keep feeding your bag periodically to keep it alive. The mojo bag is worn, but hidden from sight. It may also be hidden somewhere in the house, because if someone else touches the bag that could kill its spirit.

Dragons's Blood Ink

Use Dragon's blood ink to write in your own Book of Shadows. The ink is also used in fire spells, where you write your wish on a piece of paper or a light colored tree bark, such as birch, and give it to the fire.

To Make Dragon's Blood Ink

1 part powdered resin from
   true *Dracaena draco*
13 parts alcohol
1 part Gum arabic

Mix the resin with the Gum arabic and then very slowly blend in the alcohol, until everything is fully dissolved. Filter through cheese cloth and bottle. For best results, do this under the waxing moon.

Other magical properties

Dragon's blood incense is said to clear negativity. A woman may burn it while sitting near an open window at night, to draw back a straying lover. Place the herb near the bed to cure impotence in a man.

The powdered resin may be strewn under carpets, in entranceways, on windowsills, and anywhere you want protection from ill wishes or negative energies. Caution: do not do this if there are infants or pets that might be harmed.

Dragon's blood belongs to Mars and is of the Fire element. It is sacred to Shiva and appropriate to use in rituals to honor him.

– ELLEN EVERT HOPMAN

LUMBERJACK FOLKLORE

Squonks and other odd critters

IN THE WOODS of Wisconsin, Michigan, and Minnesota, lumberjacks around campfires amused themselves with stories. Since they shared territory with animals, all kinds of strange beasts turned up in the tall tales. Beyond Paul Bunyan's famous Blue Ox paraded some lesser-known beasts. The Hidebehind, for instance, is often sensed, never seen. You may think  you spot it out of the corner of your eye, but even if you turn swiftly the creature is gone, hiding behind a spectral curtain. Most Hidebehinds are harmless, but some of the species may be mischievous and intervene unsuspected in human lives. Be wary of any lurking Hidebehind.

Teakettlers, on the other hand, are rarely seen, more frequently heard. They are shy, although shrill. If you should spot a small dog with stumpy legs and cat's ears, chances are you are in the presence of an actual Teakettler. This will be confirmed if it walks backwards with steam issuing from its jaws. But if you see nothing and just hear a whistling, like a boiling kettle, be assured that this critter is somewhere in your vicinity.

The sadness of Squonks

In the whole imaginary animal kingdom, Squonks are some of the strangest denizens, soggy with weeping. The "scientific" name of the Squonk is *Lacrimacorpus dissolvens*, Latin for "tear," "body" and "dissolve." You could look it up somewhere. Squonk skin is the unlikely problem. It is baggy and hangs to the ground in folds, bumpy with warts, and plops along the ground gathering twigs as the animal moves. The Squonk is so distressed by its own hideousness that it hides out in the woods and cries. Few woodsmen have actually seen a Squonk because of its hydrous defense. If the animal feels cornered, the Squonk dissolves into a puddle of bubbly tears. One legendary narrator, a certain J.P. Wentling, claims to have coaxed a Squonk into a bag. As he was carrying it home, suddenly the bag felt lighter. Inside he found only the liquid remains of the sad animal.

A couple of cats

Cats always have a show of magic in animal folklore stories. In this case we have the Splintercat (*Felynx arbordiffisus*), a large feline of legendary ferociousness. It is obsessed by beehives and honey. The Splintercat flies with reckless speed through the air and bam, bam, knocks trees with its hard forehead. The trunk splinters, the leaves wither, and it becomes a ghost tree that may or may not yield what the cat loves most. Banging its head with such force gives the animal terrific headaches, which leaves it in a chronically foul mood. Watch out for the pounce of a Splintercat, a head-on collision with this grouch is no joke.

The Cactus Cat is found on western turf, but sometimes heard in distant logging camps. Its disgraceful habits are known far and wide. The creature looks like a bobcat and is covered with spines like a porcupine. Its spikiness is particularly sharp around the legs and bushy tail. The cat prowls at night, slashing at cactuses until their juices flow onto the ground. A few nights later the Cactus Cat returns, guzzles the fermented juice and runs around drunk, crazy and shrieking all night long. Around lumberjack campfires when eerie noises are heard into the wee hours, loggers laugh, poke each other and say, "Yo, Cactus Cat."

Round up

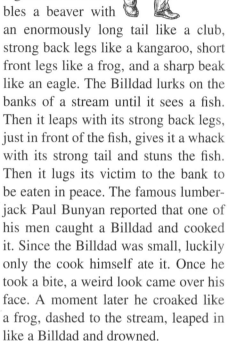

We know some fascinating details about the Billdad, a strange animal with unique fishing habits. It resembles a beaver with an enormously long tail like a club, strong back legs like a kangaroo, short front legs like a frog, and a sharp beak like an eagle. The Billdad lurks on the banks of a stream until it sees a fish. Then it leaps with its strong back legs, just in front of the fish, gives it a whack with its strong tail and stuns the fish. Then it lugs its victim to the bank to be eaten in peace. The famous lumberjack Paul Bunyan reported that one of his men caught a Billdad and cooked it. Since the Billdad was small, luckily only the cook himself ate it. Once he took a bite, a weird look came over his face. A moment later he croaked like a frog, dashed to the stream, leaped in like a Billdad and drowned.

One particular animal has a variety of names, depending on what fibber — oops, mythologist, is telling the story. The critter's most defining identity is Sidehill Gouger, but lumberjacks also refer to Sidewinder, Hunkus, Rickaboo Racker. It's a critter genetically adapted for running around hillsides, having legs shorter on one side and only able to travel in circles.

Several sightings of the elusive Hoop Snake have been alleged along the Michigan-Wisconsin border in the St. Croix River Valley. When ready to strike, the reptile can clutch the tail in its mouth and roll toward prey like a wheel. At the last second, the Hoop Snake straightens out and skewers the victim with its venomous tail. Anyone who sees a snake roll into a hoop should make a dash and hide behind a tree. Then the deadly strike will hit the tree, which will instantly die of the venom.

The Joint Snake is even more of a menace as it persists in life and eternal return to the attack. If this snake is killed with cuts of a knife or axe, the pieces simply fly together and renew the venomous action. The Joint Snake just keeps on keeping on.

Hoaxes

Sometimes pranksters turn up with such creative stories that the spoofs become legendary. So with the Hodag, "discovered" in Rhinelander, Wisconsin, in 1893 and proclaimed in local papers. It had "the head of a frog, the grinning face of a giant elephant, thick short legs set off by huge claws, the back of a dinosaur, and a long tail with spears at the end." The report was cooked up by Eugene Shepard, a well-known timberman and joker. Shepard gathered a group of locals to capture the terrifying beast.

The hunters reported that only dynamite would kill the Hodag, the last of its kind. They did the deed and sent photographs to the media — a group of men surrounding a huge black blob, the charred remains. "It was the fiercest, strangest, most frightening monster ever to set razor-sharp claws on earth," Shepard declared. "It became extinct after its main food source, all-white bulldogs, became scarce in the area."

The Furry Trout, a pretty good hoax, swam into legend through a grammatical misunderstanding. A seventeenth-century Scottish immigrant's letter home referred to the abundant "furried animals and fish" in the New World. Excited relatives asked him to procure a specimen of the "furried fish," so the mischievous Scot obliged and made one up. A century later word of the Furry Trout had taken on a life of its own. According to the later version, the waters in the Great Lakes area were so cold that a species of trout evolved with thick coats of fur to maintain body heat. And yet another theory exists, claiming that the Furry Trout resulted from four jugs of hair tonic spilled into the Arkansas River.

— Barbara Stacy

Legends and Magic of the Sea

Davy Jones and the Flying Dutchman

ALTHOUGH Davy Jones stars in Disney's *Pirates of the Caribbean* films, his legacy isn't merely a pirate story. The fearsome octopus-faced captain of the infamous ghost ship, The Flying Dutchman, in the *Pirates* film franchise, actually enjoys a longtime connection with the ocean's elusive and irresistible magic. Davy Jones belongs to all sailors and to everyone else who is lured and charmed by deep waters. For centuries, there has been a personified spirit of the sea called Davy Jones. Some believe "Jones" to be a corruption of the name Jonah. In the famous Bible story, Jonah's shipmates, blaming him for their misfortunes, tossed him overboard. For three days and three nights, Jonah survived in the belly of a whale, emerging alive.

Demon of the Seas

In sailors' lore, Jonah became associated with bad luck at sea. Davy Jones  might actually derive from 'Devil Jonah'—a demon of the seas. Stormy weather and other misfortunes at sea were attributed to Devil Jonah, with "devil" being a euphemism for Davy, Taffy, Dewi: all evil spirits and thieves of luck.

David Jones is also a very common Welsh name. Saint David, the patron saint of Wales, is invoked by sailors for safe passage and deliverance. Davy Jones became an abbreviation for their heartfelt prayers.

Press gangs and pirates

"Jones Ale is Newe" was a popular ballad in 1594 London. The song warned of a treacherous pub owner named Davy Jones, who would incapacitate unwary patrons with drugs or alcohol, and then sell them. These unfortunates were collected from Jones' ale cellar by press gangs: thugs who forced men into military or shipboard service against their will. Victims would awaken far out at sea, unwilling guests of Davy Jones. To be 'sailing with Davy Jones' came to mean sailing with Death and unable to return home.

In the 1630s, a real pirate named David Jones skulked around the Indian Ocean. He is credited with inventing the fearsome practice of walking the plank. His victims ended up at the bottom of the sea. Hence going to Davy Jones' Locker meant to be dead.

Literary references

The name Davy Jones appeared in print for the first time in 1726 in reference to a demon of the sea. Daniel Defoe mentioned Davy Jones in a phrase from his book, *The Four Years Voyages of Capt. George Roberts*. It's a reference to burials at sea and talks about tossing "them all into Davy Jones's Locker…"

In 1751, Davy is mentioned again in *The Adventures of Young Peregrine Pickle* by Tobias Smollett. Chapter 15 reads, "I'll be damned if it was not Davy Jones himself. I know him by his saucer eyes, his three rows of teeth and tail, and the blue smoke that came out of his nostrils." Furthermore, according to Smollett's character, "This same Davy Jones, according to the mythology of sailors, is the fiend that presides over all spirits of the deep, and is often seen in various shapes, perching among the rigging on the eve of hurricanes, ship-wrecks, and other disasters to which sea-faring life is exposed, warning the devoted wretch of death and woe."

By 1803, the nautical slang of sailors around the globe spoke of Davy Jones' Locker, meaning the bottom of the ocean. In 1824, Washington Irving writes of Davy Jones in his *Adventures of the Black Fisherman*, saying:

"He came, said he, and he went in a storm; he came in the night and he went in the night; he came nobody knows where.

For aught I know he has gone to sea once more on his chest; though it is a thousand pities, added he, if he has gone to Davy Jones' locker."

Robert Louis Stevenson's classic novel *Treasure Island*, published in 1883, has numerous Jones references. Stevenson coined the phrase, 'in the name of Davy Jones.'

Captain Hook, in *Peter Pan and Wendy* by J.M. Barrie, also invokes Davy Jones. The sinister Hook sings: "Yo ho, yo ho the frisky plank. You walk along it so, till it goes down and you go down, to Davy Jones below. "

Even the United States Navy honors the tradition of Davy Jones in the lyrics of the official song, "Anchors Aweigh." The current version, adopted in the 1920s, says: "…Anchors aweigh, Sail on to victory and sink their bones to Davy Jones, hooray!"

A 2006 ballad, "The Legend of Davy Jones" by David Jeremiah perpetuates the tradition. It begins:
"Some say he steers a spectral ship
That's ghostly, grey and grand,
He's doomed to sail the seven seas,
And ne'er set foot on land,
And if you chance to see him,
You'll soon be dead from fright,
So sailors tell their children,
On a dark and stormy night"

Davy's long and colorful history continues to evolve and grow. It's now being embellished by hooking Davy up with the story of *The Flying Dutchman*. Jeremiah's poem, along with Disney's *Pirates of the Caribbean* film series, seems to be the first reference to Davy Jones as the captain of a ghostly sailing vessel.

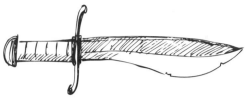

A haunted ghost ship

The Flying Dutchman, a shadowy, spectral sailing vessel, has been observed at sea since at least the seventeenth century. Said to carry a ne'er do well crew of rogues and deadbeats, it tends to appear in the fog or emerge from the edge of a storm. The sighting is a negative omen, a sure sign of impending doom. Today, the Dutchman's story has become a collective name for all haunted ships, though originally, it hailed from a very different port in nautical lore.

Medieval seamen whispered about a Captain Falkenburg, who was so skilled at dice that he bragged that he could even beat the devil. Not being one to back down from a challenge, the Evil One offered to play for his soul. The two turned out to be equals at dice and Falkenburg is said to be sailing the North Sea yet, awaiting Judgment Day and still tossing the dice.

Captain Bernard Fokke, a seventeenth century Dutchman, is thought to have been another inspiration for the endless voyage. Fokke could make the journey from Holland to Java with such speed that he was accused of being in league with the devil.

Sailing until Doomsday

Another tale is shared about a Captain Van Der Decken. In 1641, he was returning to Holland following a really productive voyage to the Far East. Sailing around the tip of Africa, near the Cape of Good Hope, Van Der Decken was deep in reverie, hatching a plan about a financial settlement with his employer, the Dutch East India Company.

He was anticipating an early payment to offer his hardworking crew and didn't see a bank of dark clouds looming on the horizon. A lookout shrieked in terror. They'd sailed right into the heart of a fearsome storm. Despite his most skilled efforts, the ship still crashed into the rocky Cape.

Van Der Decken refused to accept that death was imminent for all on board. He shouted out a curse and vowed to sail until doomsday. The devil is reputed to have heard the cry and granted the wish. George Barrington's 1795 volume, *Barrington's Voyage To Botany Bay* mentions encountering the Flying Dutchman.

Sightings

Among the most credible and famous sightings comes from Prince George of Wales, the future King George VII. He was on a three year voyage with his tutor on a Royal Navy ship, along with his brother, Prince Albert Victor. On July 11, 1881, along with the lookout, they all saw the Flying Dutchman. Prince George recorded these observations:

"A strange red light as of a phantom ship all aglow, in the midst of which the mast, spars and sails of a brig 200 yards distant stood out in strong relief."

The lookout accidentally fell and died shortly after, but fortunately the royal family survived the curse.

Sailors on the high seas have insisted that they've seen the Dutchman and his ship, even into the twenty-first century. The sinister ghostly ship was observed by a German submarine crew during World War II. The Dutchman's saga has extended to Holland, Michigan, where he is the official mascot of Hope College.

Theatrical productions

In one theatrical production, the Dutchman's captain is permitted to go ashore once each century to seek the company of a lady. A Wagnerian opera is more generous, allowing the captain a romantic encounter once every seven years. In the Disney version, Davy Jones, as captain of the Flying Dutchman, consorts with the Greek goddess Calypso.

Today contemporary travelers have a long standing invitation to keep company with the Dutchman. All KLM (Royal Dutch Airlines) aircraft have "The Flying Dutchman" lettered on the fuselage in a good humored tribute to the colorful legends about their countryman.

– ELAINE NEUMEIER

Reincarnation and Past Life Regression

Another chance to get it right

"WELL, this life looks like pretty much of a wash-out. Maybe I could pin my hopes on the next…" sighed a rather sad-faced, middle-aged gentleman. This poignant remark was overheard at a large, well-attended conference about past-life regression and reincarnation held in Chicago some years ago. A variety of workshops and meditation sessions were offered, which explored how to recall and understand past-life experiences. The idea was that choices made in the past might explain present circumstances and reveal clues about prospects for future incarnations. The gentleman who had spoken was a participant who felt he had very little to be happy about regarding his present circumstances. Like many of those in attendance, he longed to know why life is as it is and sought answers.

The belief in the rebirth of the soul in successive bodies was embraced in ancient Greece, India, and among many Native American nations. The Pythagoreans and Orphics of Greece believed that each soul was reborn several times. Finally, by living a good life, the soul would grow more refined and purified. The Hindu faith teaches that leading a life of virtue and goodness will be rewarded by rebirth in a higher form and better circumstances. Other peoples believe that the souls of those who have passed away are reborn into the same tribe or family. It is thought that even animals and supernatural beings can come back, born into higher or lower life forms.

The Vedic scriptures teach that the god Vishnu was reborn in the bodies of several deserving mortals who became avatars. The Caribou Eskimo tribe believes that the moon helps the dead return to Earth as human beings, fish, birds, or other animals. After a seal hunt, the Eskimos will sometimes hold mourning rites. This is to assure that the seals killed will be reborn to be caught again and again. The Native Americans of the Southwest believe that supernatural beings called kachina return as deer. Other Native Americans have a tradition that those who have passed away return as corn, tobacco, beans, or squash, in order to nurture the living. Many Pagan traditions also teach that the soul returns to Earth again, after a time of rest in the Summerland.

Arising refreshed

Famous people who have embraced reincarnation include Salvador Dali, William Blake, Arthur Conan Doyle,

Henry Ford, Henry David Thoreau, Pearl Buck, General George Patton, and Charles Darwin, as well as many others. At age twenty-two, Benjamin Franklin hinted at his views on the subject by writing his own witty epitaph.

The Body of B. Franklin
Printer,
Like the Cover of an Old Book,
Its Contents Torn Out
And
Stripped of its Lettering & Gilding
Lies Here
Food for Worms.
But The Book Shall Not Be Lost,
For it Will be as He Believed
Appear Once More
In a New and More Elegant Edition
Revised and Corrected
By The Author

In a letter to a friend, many years later, when he was eighty years of age, Franklin wrote "I look upon death as necessary to the constitution as sleep. We shall arise refreshed in the morning."

Proving past lives

The certainty of reincarnation isn't easy to prove. Sometimes old birth records can verify a long-ago lifetime to which one can relate, but this remains largely a matter of faith. The strongest support comes from an inner acceptance of what feels true. In addition, numerous instances of people recalling details about previous lives, showing inexplicable aptitudes or possessing knowledge that would otherwise be impossible to acquire support the idea of having lived before.

Astrologers will examine retrograde planets in the natal horoscope for insights into old business hanging on from a past life. In esoteric astrology, the sun sign is the soul itself, while the moon sign describes the emotional remembering of the soul. The moon sign also suggests the location of past lives.

Regressive hypnosis is a popular technique used to pursue past life study. A hypnotist trained in past life regression will guide the subject to explore the scene of an important past life while in a light trance state. After undergoing hypnosis and examining the past lives experienced, great insight can be gained. Afterward, the subject might be encouraged to visit the actual locations of other lives. It can also be helpful to watch films, collect pictures, music, recipes, or art, which reflect the time and place of the past life. Record dreams and impressions that occur after the regression for further study. A genuine past life will grow in detail and clarity as time passes, whereas a dream tends to fade.

For those unable or unwilling to try formal regression with a therapist, here is a simple technique for self-hypnosis, which often works well. While drifting off to sleep, visualize yourself boarding a train. Find a comfortable seat and settle in. Let the train move backwards into the scene of a significant past life. Be patient; try this for several nights. Keep a notebook handy to record impressions and recollections upon awakening.

– GRANIA LING

PLATONIC INFLUENCE

THE Renaissance embraced the Classical culture that hadn't existed for over a millennium. Alongside art, music, and sculptural nudity, one thing that epitomized the Classical Age was the practice of philosophical inquiry.

As classical works of the Graeco-Roman era were translated and disseminated, many Renaissance Christians were surprised to find that the writings of ancient Pagans contained hints of monotheism. In addition, morals and virtues were discovered within these works — many written centuries before the death of Christ — that were considered by the Church and its adherents to be "Christian" in nature. The more they researched and read, the more these Christians agreed with many of the ideas and postulates of ancient philosophy. As an added bonus, they found that many Church fathers of late antiquity had also agreed with these ancient authors. This gave many students of the occult loopholes, which could, at least, theoretically, justify their mystical and magical practices.

"So concerning the whole Heaven or World — let us call it whatsoever name may be most acceptable to it — we must ask the question which, it is agreed, must be asked at the outset if inquiry concerning anything: Has it always been, without any source of beginning or has it come to be, starting from some beginning? It has come to be, for it can be seen and touched and it has body, and all such things are sensible and as we saw, sensible thing, that are to be apprehended by belief together with sensation, are things that become and can be generated. But again, that which becomes, we say, must necessarily become by the agency of some cause. The maker and father of this universe it is a hard task to find, and having found him it would be impossible to declare him to all mankind." – Plato, *Timaeus*.

The above passage comes from the most influential and important of Plato's dialogues, at least where Renaissance occultism is concerned. *Timaeus* not only bespoke of a grand architect of the universe – the Demiurge, who Christians would immediately deem to be none other than God the Father, Creator of Heaven and Earth in the Book of Genesis, but also laid out an entire celestial cosmology, which could be, to the Renaissance magician, manipulated through the implementation of mystical formulae.

"Let us rather say that the world is like, above all things, to that Living Creature of which all other creatures, severally and in their families, are parts. For that embraces and contains within itself all the intelligible living creatures, just as this world contains ourselves and all other creatures that have been formed as things visible. For the god, wishing to make this world most nearly like that intelligible thing which is best and in every way complete, fashioned it as a single visible living creature, containing within itself all living things whose nature is of the same order." – *Timaeus*

Thus, God, the grand architect of the universe, created the world to be singular and perfect, a true representation of divinity itself or so Renaissance Christians interpreted this text, as Plato, a polytheist, had a different attitude concerning this "god." The world of *Timaeus* and ostensibly that of the Christians interpreting the text was perfect and good, being fashioned by this mighty divine creator God found within the pages of Genesis.

Timaeus held many gems of wisdom for the more practical occultists of the Renaissance. For example, the number four, holding many secrets and nuances to the mystically-minded, revealed itself most importantly (at first), as the four classical elements of antiquity, which Plato made certain to include in his cosmogony.

"Now that which comes to be must be bodily, and so visible and tangible; and nothing can be visible without fire, or tangible without something solid, and nothing is solid without earth. Hence the god, when he began to put together the body of the universe, set about making it of fire and earth. But two things alone cannot be satisfactorily united without a third; for there must be some bond between them drawing together... Now if it had been required that the body of the universe should be a plane surface with no depth, a single mean would have been enough to connect its companions and itself; but in fact the world was to be solid in form, and solids are always conjoined, not by one mean, but by two. Accordingly the god set water and air between fire and earth, and made them so far as was possible, proportional to one another, so that as fire is to air, so is air to water, and as air is to water, so is water to earth, and thus he bound together the frame of a world visible and tangible." – *Timaeus*

Thus, not only did Plato make the four elements correspond to a geometrical format, he also established a descending order that spoke of their inherent theoretical density: Fire Air Water Earth, with Fire being the least dense of the elements and Earth being the heaviest. The four-fold nature of the world was also expounded upon by mystics in other mathematical manners. For example, the addition of the numbers one through four equal ten (1+2+3+4=10), the decad or perfect number, thus further proving, to the minds of the Hermeticists, the inherent harmony found within Plato's cosmology and subsequently, the world itself. Of course, this harmony was considered old news by the time of Plato's writing, having been professed by Pythagorean mystics centuries earlier, as the mysteries of the tetractys and decad. However, to the Hermeticists rediscovering ancient wisdom, these were profound mysteries indeed.

It should be noted that these concepts had already been adapted by Kabbalists centuries before. As Kabbalistic theory also began to penetrate the writings of the Renaissance occultists, the number four was found to correspond with the Tetragrammaton, the ineffable four-fold Hebraic name of God: YHVH (the Hebrew letters Yud-Heh-Vav-Heh, rendered by Renaissance writers as "Jehovah" and by many modern authors as "Yahweh"). Each of the four elements was associated with a letter of the Tetragrammaton, as well as one of the four theoretical Kabbalistic worlds. The additional permutations of the four that yield ten would then correspond to the ten

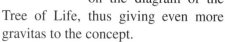

Sephirot of the Tree of Life — essentially a blueprint representation of the theoretical universe.

As Plato further spoke of the four elements as approached geometrically in the double and triple geometric proportions, yet another "sacred" number embraced by the later Hermeticists emerged: seven. If taken in order, the proportions yielded seven specific numbers: 1, 2, 3, 4, 8, 9, and 27, respectively. Also, if we take the "perfect" number 10 of any particular thing (rocks, grapes, sticks, etc.) and arrange them in an ascending shape pyramid, (following yet again the 1+2+3+4=10 arrangement), four rows result (think beer pong, for example).

Three sides and four rows thus yielded both seven and ten, further "proving" their numerical sanctity (as well as the perceived genius inherent to the ordered universe, as described by Plato) to the Renaissance occultist. The number seven was placed in an even more prominent position by Plato and the later Hermeticists, because of its correspondence to the Seven Holy Planets: Sol, Luna, Mercury, Mars, Venus, Jupiter, and Saturn. In addition, the glyph of Venus, also associated with the number seven, is the sole planetary glyph that can encompass all of the Sephirot on the diagram of the Tree of Life, thus giving even more gravitas to the concept.

"…but the inner revolution he split in six places into seven unequal circles, severally corresponding with the double and triple intervals, of each of which there were three." – *Timaeus*

As Hermetic knowledge grew, expanded, and combined with the era's Christian mysticism, specific correspondences were attributed to the numbers. Henry Cornelius Agrippa, writing in the early 16th century, in his *Three Books of Occult Philosophy*, corresponded the number 7 with particular angels, days of the week, musical notes, body parts, holes of the head (nostrils, for example), stars of the Pleiades, metals, birds, fish, mammals, stones, Roman kings, Roman hills, infernal habitations, wise men of Greece, and so forth.

This system of correspondence would not only be utilized as a mnemonic technique, but would become an integral part of Hermetic spell-casting, during the Renaissance, whether through ritual incantations, the construction of magical talismans, the summoning of spirits to perform tasks for the magician, or just about any other magical endeavor.

During the Renaissance, the practice of astrology was considered a necessity to the practitioners of Hermetic magic, in part because of the importance Plato placed upon the power of celestial bodies. This emphasis was perpetuated by the Platonists, Neo-Platonists, Kabbalists, and Hermeticists who came after. As Agrippa quipped:

"There is therefore such a kind of Spirit required to be, as it were the medium, whereby celestial souls are joined to gross bodies, and bestow upon them wonderful gifts… By this Spirit therefore every occult property is conveyed into herbs, stones, metals, and animals, through the Sun, Moon, planets, and through stars higher than the planets." –Agrippa, *Three Books of Occult Philosophy*

Each planet would subsequently have multiple terrestrial representations naturally occurring upon Earth, each one imbued to a certain extent with the "essence" of the corresponding planet in question. For example, things such as iron, jasper, garlic, wolfsbane, nettles, a crow's feather, and snake-skin would be considered to be under the dominion of Mars. Therefore, if a magician wished to cast a spell in order to succeed at a particularly martial endeavor — let's say, to emerge triumphant from a duel — he would use components that were under Mars' celestial jurisdiction. Astrological charts would likely also be implemented, in order to determine the most advantageous time for spell-casting.

"We have spoken in the foregoing chapters of the divers kinds of divinations: but this is to be noted, that all these require the use and rules of astrology, as a key most necessary for the knowledge of all secrets; and that all kinds of divinations whatsoever have their root and foundation in astrology, so as that without it they are of little or no use…" –Agrippa

– TETH MYSTERIUM

Ghost Lore from America's Oldest City

St. Augustine's haunted lighthouse

LIGHTHOUSES are lonely places and so it is no surprise that they figure prominently in the lore of hauntings. Standing in a nether land between the shore and sea, lighthouses seem to be natural portals for supernatural activity. Many credible paranormal investigators, including Joyce Elson Moore, author of *Haunt Hunter's Guide to Florida*, describe the lighthouse in St. Augustine, Florida as teeming with especially active and usually friendly ghosts. Contemporary ghost hunters carrying digital cameras and hand-held EMF (electromagnetic frequency) meters are gleeful upon finding images of spirit orbs or even full bodied apparitions and energy spikes, when exploring the lighthouse, the keeper's home, and the extensive, beautifully landscaped grounds.

When the US postal service offered a set of stamps honoring lighthouses, St. Augustine's stately black and white spiral, capped with a red topped beacon, was included. The structure is certainly among America's most impressive lighthouses. It is the oldest and perhaps the most beautiful and famous of the thirty-one lighthouses, which light up nightly and dot Florida's one-thousand miles of waterfront.

Florida's first lighthouse

Each sunset, since 1565, the shallow and treacherous inlet where the St. John's River flows into the Atlantic Ocean has had a variety of beacons aglow, projecting a measure of safety and confidence to seafarers. In 1824, the St. Augustine Lighthouse was officially recognized as Florida's first lighthouse. The current brick structure was built in 1875, replacing the older wooden buildings that had eroded with the passing of time.

At first, the light keepers — women among them — would have to climb two-hundred nineteen steps, twice daily, while lugging a heavy can, first containing tallow and later kerosene, to fuel the flame. Today, visitors are invited to lift one of the cans. Even empty, the effort is daunting. It seems unbelievably difficult to carry to the top.

In 1936, the light became electrified and, slowly, technology made navigation safer and easier. Although the lighthouse remains functional, its role has changed. It is now treasured as a popular tourist destination, historical site, and museum.

Lighthouse ghosts

During the daytime and even more so during the ghost tours offered on weekend evenings, the place has an atmosphere. A variety of presences have been perceived, linked to those who were devoted to the lighthouse and are loathe to leave it, even in death. Mary and Eliza, two sweet little girls, are among the lighthouse's most endearing ghosts. The two joined a group of beach-goers, near the turn of the last century, who were crowded into a cart, a ride that ran on tracks from the lighthouse to the sea. As it traveled quickly down an incline, the cart tipped over. The other passengers escaped, but Mary and Eliza were trapped underneath and crushed to death. The pair have lingered. Visitors report hearing Mary and Eliza's footsteps and laughter, echoing around the lighthouse grounds.

John Lienlockken, a St. Augustine handyman, mentioned many bizarre incidents he experienced when he was hired to do repairs, following an arson fire in the 1970s. Several times, he and his crew saw someone hanging from scaffolding that they had erected, only to look again and find the apparition was gone. Eventually, three workers quit, too spooked by the eerie incidents to complete the job. Jake, a neighbor, who claims to see lights flickering around the grounds at night, told John that it was probably the ghost of a vagrant, who had hanged himself in the lighthouse tower during the 1930s.

Kathleen Steward, who worked as a tour guide at the lighthouse, observed a tall, thin figure leaning over the edge at the top of the structure. She ran in, using the only entrance, noting that, for some reason, the alarm had been disconnected. The lighthouse was empty. She learned later that Mr. Andreau, a light keeper in the 1850s, who answered that physical description, had fallen to his death, while painting the first light tower. His wife assumed his duties, to support their family and herself.

Visiting the lighthouse

Whether or not a ghostly encounter is experienced, the St. Augustine Lighthouse and museum are certainly well worth visiting. It is always breezy and cool at the top with a spectacular view. The museum collection, including original furnishings, artifacts, a doll donated by one of the keeper's daughters, vintage clothes and photos, is impressive.

The Lighthouse, located on Hwy A1A, just south of downtown St. Augustine, is open daily from about 9am -7pm, depending upon the weather and the time of year. Admission costs about $10.00. Weekend ghost tours are offered from about 8:30pm to midnight; the cost is about $25.00.

– Marina Bryony

Afternoon Tea for Witchery and Steampunk

ENTHUSIASTICALLY embraced by witches of all traditions, Steampunk serves as an inspiration for the practice of magic and is a path toward the creation of a spiritual life. Pagan gatherings frequently include presentations about Steam, whose popularity has expanded over the past two decades, transforming it from an obscure literary genre into a phenomenon featuring conferences, publications, a tarot deck, costumes and accessories.

For those who have not yet encountered the delights of Steam, it is best described as "Victorian science fiction." Insight may be obtained from the writings of H.G. Wells and Jules Verne. If the future had happened in the past, it would be Steam. Think of aviator glasses, hot air balloon rides, time travel by steamboats and train, safari outfits, top hats, long skirts, waist coats, mechanical corsets, a steam-powered metal elephant, and perpetual motion clocks. The mood is Gothic and the world is brown, grey, black, and white, with only occasional splashes of color.

Themed tea parties

Despite its many interpretations, Steam always returns to a background that suggests Victorian England, where afternoon tea was essential. Witches who are also enthusiastic Steampunkers are exploring the magical possibilities of themed tea parties. Recent examples include A Mad Hatter's Tea (with all participants wearing tiny and elaborately decorated top hats), a Silent Communication Tea (featuring quiet, soulful reverie), a One Hundred Candles Tea (featuring an evening of Victorian ghost stories), and a Games Tea that revives Victorian parlor games, such as Shopkeeper, Captain's Cat or Carnelli, card games and chess.

The traditional etiquette and rituals of taking tea is an enjoyable and powerful way to begin incorporating the world of Steam into small coven meetings, as well as larger Pagan holidays.

Teatime traditions

By the 1800s, tea, once an expensive luxury, had become affordable enough that nearly every home in the United States and Western Europe had a teapot. The type of tea served — as well as the associated serving pieces — was considered a status symbol, available to both the middle and upper classes. Ideally a genteel and well-mannered mood would be set, thus pleasing and impressing those whom one wished to cultivate with the perfect tea party. The difference between just taking tea with the family versus an important social gathering lies in the elements of ritual and formality.

The tea *hour* usually spans 3:00 to 5:00 in the afternoon, although activities may extend into the evening. In that case, the gathering might be called a soiree, including singing and dancing. English Duchess, Anna of Bedford began the tea time tradition in the early 1840s. She complained of feeling weary in the afternoon, before dinner was ready. Anna's friends looked forward to the tea and cakes she offered to assuage their hunger.

Soon it was the fashion to serve tiny sandwiches and beautifully decorated little cakes, alongside tea, all on fine china, while admiring curious, interesting bric a brac, or exchanging the latest gossip. Pleasant conversation

was encouraged. Tea leaf readings and fortunetelling games might also be featured.

Teatime tools

Miss Leslie's 1849 guide, *The House Book or a Manual of Domestic Economy*, offers the specifics of pulling together the perfect tea party: a tea set with cups and saucers, a teapot and stand, sugar bowl, slop bowl, mote spoons, spoon tray, sugar nips, tea caddy or teapoy, cream pitcher, and both large and small plates. While a matching set of china is most fashionable, a mixed set of cups and saucers, called "a harlequin set" is acceptable, providing the pieces were of good quality, never paltry or mean. Cut glass bowls of preserves and ginger, as well as candles in silver candlesticks were also recommended to "lend a glow of affluence and charm."

A mote spoon is a long handled, slotted spoon for straining errant leaves from tea. Sugar nips are for removing the desired amount of sugar from a larger cone. Slop bowls were to empty the hot water used to rinse the cups before adding tea and for the dregs of remaining tea leaves. A tea caddy or teapoy was a chest or three-legged stand, displaying several kinds of tea and mixing bowls.

Square and even

During the Victorian era, many other directories and guides

were published, which emphasized the importance of propriety and form when serving tea. The gist of these is that everything — even the rugs — be set out 'square and even.' The eldest daughter or youngest married lady would pour the tea with the teapot resting near her right hand. Everything was set on the table at once; there were no separate courses.

The gracious presentation of tea would often set the tone for a desirable courtship. The social custom of extending the pinky finger probably originated when most cups had no handles. In some circles the tea from a handle-less cup would be poured into a dish or saucer, then drunk, although that practice came to be frowned upon by society.

To make tea sandwiches:
1. Remove the crusts from the bread
2. Lightly butter a slice
3. Cut it in halves or quarters, creating small square or triangle shapes.
4. Popular sandwich fillings included small quantities of cucumber, watercress, tomato, cheese, or smoked salmon.

– GRANIA LING

LITERARY REFLECTIONS AND THE VICTORIAN TEA:

"Bread and water can so easily become toast with tea." – Anonymous

"Under certain circumstances, there are few hours in life more agreeable than the hour dedicated to the ceremony known as afternoon tea."
– Henry James from his novel, *The Portrait of a Lady*

"In nothing more is the English genius for domesticity more notably declared than in the institution of this festival of afternoon tea. The mere chink of cups and saucers tunes the mind to a happy response."
– George Gissing, author of *The Private Papers of Henry Ryecroft*

"Love and scandal are the best sweeteners of tea"
– Henry Fielding, from *Love in Several Masques*

"I believe it is customary, in good society, to take some slight refreshment at five o'clock."
– Oscar Wilde, from *The Importance of Being Earnest*

"In a few minutes tea was brought. Very delicate was the china, very old the plate, very thin the bread-and-butter and very small the lumps of sugar. "
– Elizabeth Gaskell, from her novel, *Cranford*

"I just love my afternoon tea."
– Elizabeth Pepper, founder of
The Witches' Almanac

The enchanter Merlin, magician of King Arthur's Round Table, meeting the fairy Viviane in the Forest of Broceliande. After an enameled book cover, Limoges, early fifteenth century.

The Old Religion

PRETENTIONS to great antiquity — as if age testifies to something more than sheer endurance — are a hallmark of many esoteric organizations. The Freemasons, their earliest Grand Lodge dating from 1717, trace their origins back to King Solomon, if not before, while their down-market imitators, the Royal Antediluvian Order of Buffaloes, imply in their title that they pre-date Noah and the Flood. Others happily stick the word "Ancient" in front of their name, as does the Ancient and Mystical Order Rosae Crucis (AMORC), though its beginnings go back no further than 1915. (Rosicrucianism, as such, dates from 1614 when pamphlets chronicling the life of Christian Rosenkreuz began to circulate in Germany, their author a Lutheran pastor named Johann Valentin Andreae. This inconvenient detail did not deter Harvey Spencer Lewis, founder of AMORC, from claiming the movement began in 1489 BCE under the enlightened patronage of Pharaoh Thutmose III.) Meanwhile Madame Blavatsky, a hard act to follow, tirelessly maintained that the "Ancient Wisdom" she purveyed came from *The Stanzas of Dzyan*, the oldest book in the world, its teachings written on palm leaves in a long forgotten language. The Mormon revelation is modern by comparison, with Madame spared the bother of digging up gold plates like poor Joseph Smith.

All of which entitles us to treat with skepticism the claims made by early defenders of witchcraft that what they practiced was a continuation of (and thus more or less the same as) what our ancestors got up to centuries, even millennia, ago. Why do such things matter? Well, the answer is they don't. Or, rather, the historical credentials of witchcraft are of minor importance compared with the spiritual benefit it brings to those involved in it. The trouble is that a number of them, albeit fewer than before, still persist in harping on about the "old" religion, boasting how theirs is the last authentic remnant of a magical tradition scrupulously kept under wraps until now.

Putting the oomph into witchcraft

Well, not quite until now. Those of us growing up in the nineteen-fifties will remember how, by the middle of that decade, witchcraft was shedding its much-vaunted secrecy. Not only did Gerald Gardner publish two books on the subject, but, with scant regard for his own reputation or that of witchcraft, exposed himself, often literally, to the scurrilous attentions of the Sunday press. At school, I remember being shown a copy of *The People* — my parents were too high-minded to buy it — which spoke of a "repulsive pagan sect" and, as if to prove the point, displayed a picture of Gardner with two younger companions, all three naked, but with none of the oomph we boys expected. It would be Maxine and Alex Sanders who put the oomph into witchcraft. But that was years later.

Whether our ancestors possessed it, we shall never know. Come to that, we don't even know if they took their clothes off when performing the rituals ascribed to them by Gardner. Still, most experts agree that the ancient Celts did probably go into battle wearing no more than a quick dab of woad, so it's not inconceivable that they stripped off on other occasions as well. (Literary and archaeological evidence suggests that for most of the time they stayed covered up, the women in tunics and men in trousers, with both sharing a fondness for plaid and lots of costume jewelry.) As Gerald Gardner was a dedicated naturist, even joint owner of a nudist club, it is reasonable to suppose that his personal preferences account in part for the nudity he required of his followers. I say "in part" because arguments in favour of nudity certainly exist, though this is not the place to explore them.

"Wiccan" religion

A bigger challenge is the job of assessing whether Gardner's claims about the antiquity of witchcraft or, rather, his version of it, are justified. Today few people, witches included, would fully endorse the claim in his book *Modern Witchcraft*, (1954), that what he described in it was the remnant of an old religion secretly practiced for centuries. Certainly there is no support for that view among historians and folklorists, apart from Margaret Murray, who at the age of ninety was persuaded to write the book's introduction. The paucity of historical evidence is in contrast to the plentiful reports we have of ceremonial magicians and what they believed or got up to centuries ago. Here, it is permissible to speak of a "tradition" even if it was no more than a hotchpotch of Neo-Platonism, Kabbalah, astrology, numerology and material brought back from the East by merchants and Crusaders.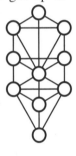

By contrast nowhere in the historical record, apart from some disputed sources in Italy, do we find evidence of a Wiccan "religion," by which I mean a set of beliefs and cultic practices preserved within small communities and secretly handed down over the centuries. Of course those who defend its existence might point out, not unreasonably, that the absence of hard evidence is unsurprising, given the element of secrecy involved. True enough, but still not proof it ever existed. On top of which it seems improbable that a clandestine religion, especially one of more than local significance, would have evaded the attention of diligent researchers and historians. It is noteworthy, too, that not even their most ruthless persecutors accused witches of belonging to a religion of their own or even subscribing to a consistent set of beliefs. True, they were held to have sold their souls to the devil, even worshipped him on occasion, just as the Knights Templar allegedly worshipped Baphomet — who, like the arch fiend Satan, bears more than a passing resemblance to the Horned God — but this was viewed as a repudiation of Christianity, rather than allegiance to a completely different religion.

One curious detail

What is also indisputable is that historical scholarship tells us little about what witches actually believed, if indeed they shared a common belief, and this despite an abundance of information about what they did or, more often the case, what they were accused of doing. That the majority were simple country folk, most of them illiterate, further deprives us of the kind of information their more erudite contemporaries, writers on magic like Pietro d'Abano, Trithemius, Agrippa, and Johannes Wierus were only too willing to impart. Still, one curious detail does merit attention, even though it involves only hearsay evidence and is nowadays encountered less often than it was.

It concerns the number of individuals who claim to have been introduced to witchcraft by family members, more often than not by their grandmother. Known as "hereditary" witches, a badge of pride for many, some talk of a formal initiation, as did Alex Sanders, for example, while others, among them Robert Cochrane, claim to have learned of their heritage by chance or been informed of it by a parent or other close relation. Few can match Ruth Wynn Owen, sometime actress and friend of the poet, Dylan Thomas, whose father came from Anglesey. She proclaimed herself heir to a tradition stretching back all the way to Brân, alias Bendigeidfran or Brân the Blessed, a superhuman character in the *Mabinogion*, whose head supposedly lies buried at the White Mount in London. Today her teachings, much influenced by the books of Margaret Murray and Sir James Fraser's *Golden Bough*, as well as Welsh mythology, are still cherished – she died in 2001 – by a group calling itself (with disregard for correct Welsh usage) Y Plant Bran.

Hereditary witches

Another hereditary witch was Eleanor Bone, one of Gardner's High Priestesses and an influential figure in her own right, who maintained that prior to her introduction to Gardner she had belonged to a group of witches in Cumbria. Perhaps she had, yet no matter how persuasive such claims may be, they remain impossible to verify and do little to convince the impartial observer that the Craft existed prior to (and thus independently of) individuals like Gardner, with knowledge of it passed from one generation to the next. Still, as I said earlier, with witches increasingly self-confident and the Craft judged, quite rightly, for what it is, not by where it came from, fewer such claims are heard nowadays.

For me what is striking about such anecdotes is how many involve women reputed to be Welsh. Of these none is more notorious than the Mrs. Bibby, who, according to his biographer, initiated a bemused Alex Sanders in her kitchen one afternoon, the two of them stark naked and he just seven years old. That happened not far from the village of Betws-y-Coed, claimed by some, usually visitors charmed by its waterfall and sylvan landscape, to be the final refuge of the *tylwyth têg* or fairy folk. From a village close by, also named Betws, came the unfortunate Gwen Ferch Elis, tried for witchcraft at Chester assizes in 1594 and subsequently hanged, one of only five people in Wales executed for that offence. Betws-y-Coed is also where the founder of an American organization, the Dynion Mwyn, claims to have learned "The Old Ways" from a local wise man named (improbably) Taliesin Einion Vawr. Calling himself

Rhuddlwm Gwawr, he went on to establish the Church of *Y Tylwyth Têg* or Church of the Fairies in Maryland. Oh yes, and the village was home also to Dr. Edward Bach, famous for his Flower Remedies. Personally, I've never much cared for the place.

Popular consciousness

Reports of this kind have persuaded me that far from inventing the whole Wiccan package, as his critics never tire of maintaining, Gerald Gardner, originally a member of a New Forest coven, did indeed have access to remnants of a tradition of remarkable antiquity. From these sparse resources he drew whatever he could, but felt no qualms about embellishing it to suit his taste. Certainly there seem grounds for accepting that an attachment to the sanctity of the natural world, something typically Pagan, did survive for two thousand years, in what the Germans (who have a knack for such things) call the *Volksseele* or popular consciousness. Seldom, if ever, did it consolidate into a coherent religious system, but among country dwellers or at least a minority of them, it continued to find expression in rituals like those I heard of as a boy growing up in Wales, as well as in ancient practices, deemed superstitious, that survive to this day. Typical of them is the reverence shown towards places formerly sacred to the old gods but long "Christianized" by the Church, even endowed with a new saintly patron, though old god and new saint often turn out to be one and the same.

One example familiar to me lies within easy walking distance of my home, though "easy" may be the wrong word, as it is reached only after an arduous climb. It involves what is held to be the grave of Taliesin, the 6th century Welsh poet, but is, in fact, a Bronze Age monument dating from at least 1000 BCE. Such was the poet's reputation that, over the years, people began attributing to him supernatural powers, the fate also of the Roman poet Virgil, turning him into a powerful wizard and prophet. Taliesin even appears on a list of Celtic deities published on an American website for Wiccans, though, in fairness, acknowledgement is made of his historical existence as well. Meanwhile, a century ago, again in America, the architect Frank Lloyd Wright paid his own tribute to the poet by naming his home in Wisconsin after him, as well as a second residence, Taliesin West, which he later built near Scottsdale, Arizona. (Lloyd Wright was no stranger to esoteric matters, having studied the works of Blavatsky and been a friend of the Russian guru, George Gurdjieff, while also sharing with Rudolf Steiner, founder of Anthroposophy, a commitment to what both called "organic" architecture.) It seems fitting therefore that on the dozen or so occasions I have visited the poet's reputed burial place high above the village that today bears his name, I have found votive offerings reverently placed there.

Pagan tendencies

Such behaviour is indicative of the Pagan tendency to invest natural objects or features of the landscape with supernatural meaning, just as the ancient Celts held certain places sacred and left there votive offerings like those found in abundance at Llyn Cerrig Bach on Anglesey. This sense of "place" was profoundly important to them, as it still is to many country folk. Certain animals, too, were venerated, doubtless because they typified virtues which, because admirable in human beings, have necessarily to be common to the gods as well. Thus the bear, admired for its strength, tenacity and courage, was linked to the goddess Artio, a name related to the Celtic word for bear (Welsh *arth*, as found in the derivative Arthur, "the once and future king"), while Epona, derived from the word for horse (modern Welsh: *ebol* = colt or foal) was associated with fertility and healing, especially healing springs. Noteworthy, too, is that Epona, one of the few Celtic deities formally adopted by Rome – her feast day was 18 December – was often identified with the Mother Goddess herself.

What is undeniable is that in modern witchcraft, as in every other religion, there are elements begged, borrowed, or stolen from somewhere else. That critics of modern witchcraft point to elements attributable to the Hermetic

Order of the Golden Dawn, to Aleister Crowley and even, purportedly, to the Scottish Presbyterian Hymn Book, should cause us no unease whatever. The only question we need ask is – do they work? If they do, then so much the better.

Mirror of our ancestors

What is undeniable is that because of its Pagan commitment, witchcraft may justifiably claim to represent the Old Religion, traces of it discernible in folk-lore and, indeed, in the heart of anyone who has ever paused to gaze up at the moon and suddenly — mysteriously — felt loved. Whether its practices exactly mirror those of our primitive ancestors is uncertain, even disputable, but also sublimely irrelevant. These after all are but the expression of a religious or spiritual commitment and, as such, they may, indeed *should*, be adapted to satisfy current preferences. If in order to accomplish this, witches have borrowed bits and pieces from the Golden Dawn, from Freemasonry, from Aleister Crowley, from Charles Leland's *Aradia*, from Robert Graves or from anywhere else, then so what? All that counts is the effect such disparate elements have on us individually, on our fellow celebrants and on those supra-sensible realities we aspire to work with.

Above all, do they bring us closer to the gods? Or, this being witchcraft, do they bring the gods closer to us? If the answer is yes, then the rest doesn't matter. Neither do the foibles and all-too-human weaknesses, far outweighed by their strengths, of those pioneers who revived or reinvented witchcraft over half a century ago.

– DAVID CONWAY

TEN CANDLES
AND A BUNDLE OF RUE

GROWING UP Latino, as I did, in an urban setting, frequenting the local botanica was not only a common event, in many instances, it was a necessity. You see, in our house, not only did we pray to the household statue of the Virgin, we also washed our floors with luck-drawing washes, stashed herbs well-hidden from sight by the front door to draw in blessings and ward off evil spirits, and regularly offered white candles at the family *boveda* (an altar for spiritual and familial ancestors).

The local botanica is an interesting place to visit. The literal translation of the word *botanica* is "herb store" and so you might think that the fare encountered there would be a bunch of herbs, perhaps for cooking. In fact, a botanica is a unique blend of spiritual supply store, apothecary selling both fresh and dried herbs, and home to a local psychic, who can advise which of the many products to acquire, in order to advance the mundane and spiritual needs of your life.

Mom, Marisol, and Manny

My mother was always sure to tend to all of our family's needs and so, every once in a while, she would pack us all up and off we would go to one of her favorite botanicas for the requisite *consulta* (consultation or reading). Invariably, this meant that various products would need to be purchased in order to resolve issues that were pointed out during the reading or to help nudge along the foretold blessings about to come into our lives.

Upon walking into the botanica, Mom was always greeted by Marisol with a huge smile and an offer of *café con leche* that was served alongside a good amount of local gossip, comparisons of child rearing woes, and other chatter about neighborhood goings-on. They would chat until Manny, the resident *Santero* (orisha priest), was done with his previous client. He was always pleasant and always dressed in the blue hues of his patron, Yemaya.

Mom was then ushered into a little room at the back of the botanica. The curtain was drawn and the hum of hushed-toned prayers began, as Manny spoke to his *santos*, telling them who was sitting in front of him, and asking them to give clear advice. We kids were never allowed into the room where the *consulta* took place. I always wondered what was going on — the rattling of shells and the soft voice of my mother asking questions, never quite loud enough to allow us to hear, but always imbued with warmth and concern.

Santa Barbara and Chango

While Mom had her consultation with the saints, Marisol allowed us to rummage in the botanica's aisles. I had a special attraction to the statues, especially those of Santa Barbara. Marisol loved to tell me the stories of the saints and how they were the masks of the gods themselves. She would tell me that I was the child of Chango, the god who lived behind the mask of Saint Barbara.

My young mind jubilantly sipped on the knowledge imparted by Marisol. She showed me a statue of Chango, a seated, dark figure wearing a gold crown. She told me that Chango was a king and that all of his children enjoyed being treated like royalty, to which she added a wink and a smile. She showed me his special house, known as a *batea* (a wooden bowl with a top) and his *oshe* or double headed axe.

On one very special visit, Marisol gave me a rock that was in the shape of a tear drop. She told me how Chango descended to Earth as lightning during thunderstorms and would leave behind rocks known as *piedras de rayo*. I was enthralled to receive such a special gift. It was from that day that Marisol and Manny would call me *Changosito*, "Little Chango." To this day, even as a grown man with a wife and children, many call out to me, "*Como anda Changosito* (How's it going, Changosito)?"

Sacred Prescriptions

When Manny and my mother were finished, the curtain to the back room would open. I would hear my mother give thanks to Manny with a warm full throated, "*Bendicion Padrino*" (Bless me, Godfather) to which he would eagerly respond, "*Santo*" (You are blessed).

Manny would have a brief discussion with Marisol, advising her of the *resuelvos* (resolving remedies) that the *santos* had given. From that point, Marisol would take care of Mom, as Manny tended to the next *consulta*. Marisol would quickly and with eager chatter, punctuated with strong advice, begin to put together a package of the necessities the *santos* had dictated through Manny. Acting as both order clerk and pharmacist, Marisol filled the order provided by the doctor. My mother would memorize the instructions provided to her and we would leave the botanica with a brown paper bag full of supplies.

Baths, Whites, Memories

Back at home, there were baths to be taken to hasten the blessings that the *santos* advised were surely on their way. Sometimes there was a bath for each of us, the raw ingredients packaged in individually marked little brown bags. Mom would bathe us with the herbs; afterwards dressing us in white clothing. Often, as we rested in our whites, Mom would light a candle to the Virgin and pray softly.

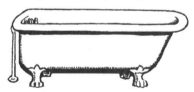

Sometimes, as we rested, Mom would offer coffee and cigars to the ancestors at the *boveda* or speak to Elegua, the little guardian that lived at our door, serving him sweets, a small amount of chili peppers, and spraying him with *aguardiente*, the firewater drink preferred by the saints.

It has been a long time since I have seen Marisol or Manny, but the knowledge that they imparted and the love for the *santos* has stayed with me. Mom's picture now lives on the *boveda*. I remember the magic and blessings that lived in our house and that now lives in the very core of my being. So, the next time you pass by a botanica, take note that this is sacred space, where lives are cared for.

– DEMETRIUS SANTIAGO

The Lady & the Lion

ONCE UPON a time there was a father who had three daughters. One day, before he went on a trip, he asked them what presents they wanted him to bring back. The two elder daughters wanted jewelry, which was simple enough for the father to get. But the youngest wanted a singing, soaring lark. Before his return, the father had bought the jewelry, but be had not found a lark. As he was passing through a dark forest, he spied one in a tree, climbed up and caught it. At that very moment a lion, howling with rage, came bounding out. "How dare you take my lark," he roared. "Prepare to die!" The man begged to be spared and the lion let him go, on the condition that his youngest daughter be given to him.

When the man returned home, there was great wailing as he told his story. But the youngest daughter did not fear and went alone into the forest. There she was met by the lion, who took her to his castle, where other lions dwelt. He was a prince under a spell, and took his human form at night, as did his companions. The lion and the maid fell in love and lived happily together.

One day the lion told the maid that her eldest sister was about to be married, and gave her permission to visit home if she so wanted. The maid refused, unless the lion would come with her.

He told her that he dared not, for were a single ray of light to touch him, he would turn into a dove and be forced to fly about the world for seven years The maid promised she would protect him from the light.

The lion went to the wedding feast, but, as fate would have it, even through the maid tried to shield him from the light, a beam touched him. He turned into a dove and flew away. For seven years the maid endured great hardship trying to find him. Then she found that, human again, he had married an evil princess, who had taken his memory from him. She went to the princess, who envied the maid's gown, which had been given to her by the sun during her wanderings. The princess asked the maid if she would sell it. The maid said she would give it only if she were allowed to enter the prince's room that night. The bargain was struck, but the princess put a drug in his drink. When the maid entered the prince's room, she was unable to rouse him.

The next day, the maid showed the princess three eggs which the moon had given her during her wanderings. She broke them open and out ran three golden chicks. The princess wanted them, and the maid gave them on the condition that she again be allowed into the prince's room. But that night the prince did not drink the drug, so when the maid was let into his chamber, he recognized her and told her how he had been enslaved by the princess.

Now the princess's father was a powerful sorcerer, so the prince and the maid quietly slipped from the palace. They mounted a griffin which bore them over the Red Sea. When the beast became tired, the maid dropped a nut the night wind had given her. At once, a tall nut tree grew from the water and the griffin was able to rest in its branches for the night. In the morning, he returned the prince and the maid home safely and they lived in peace and contentment for the rest of their lives.

– THE BROTHERS GRIMM

MOON GARDENING

BY PHASE

Sow, transplant, bud and graft   *Plow, cultivate, weed and reap*

NEW	First Quarter	FULL	Last Quarter	NEW
Plant above-ground crops with outside seeds, flowering annuals.	Plant above-ground crops with inside seeds.	Plant root crops, bulbs, biennials, perennials.		Do not plant.

BY PLACE IN THE ZODIAC

Fruitful Signs

Cancer — Most favorable planting time for all leafy crops bearing fruit above ground. Prune to encourage growth in Cancer.

Scorpio — Second only to Cancer, a Scorpion Moon promises good germination and swift growth. In Scorpio, prune for bud development.

Pisces — Planting in the last of the Watery Triad is especially effective for root growth.

Taurus — The best time to plant root crops is when the Moon is in the sign of the Bull.

Capricorn — The Earthy Goat Moon promotes the growth of rhizomes, bulbs, roots, tubers and stalks. Prune now to strengthen branches.

Libra — Airy Libra may be the least beneficial of the Fruitful Signs, but is excellent for planting flowers and vines.

Barren Signs

Leo — Foremost of the Barren Signs, the Lion Moon is the best time to effectively destroy weeds and pests. Cultivate and till the soil.

Gemini — Harvest in the Airy Twins; gather herbs and roots. Reap when the Moon is in a sign of Air or Fire to assure best storage.

Virgo — Plow, cultivate, and control weeds and pests when the moon is in Virgo.

Sagittarius — Plow and cultivate the soil or harvest under the Archer Moon. Prune now to discourage growth.

Aquarius — This dry sign of Air is perfect for ground cultivation, reaping crops, gathering roots and herbs. It is a good time to destroy weeds and pests.

Aries — Cultivate, weed, and prune to lessen growth. Gather herbs and roots for storage.

Consult our Moon Calendar pages for phase and place in the zodiac circle. The Moon remains in a sign for about two-and-a-half days. Match your gardening activity to the day that follows the Moon's entry into that zodiac sign.

The MOON Calendar

is divided into zodiac signs rather than the more familiar Gregorian calendar.

2015

2016

Bear in mind that new projects should be initiated when the Moon is waxing (from dark to full). When the Moon is on the wane (from full to dark), it is a time for storing energy and the wise person waits.

Please note that Moons are listed by day of entry into each sign. Quarters are marked, but as rising and setting times vary from one region to another, it is advisable to check your local newspaper, library or planetarium.
The Moon's Place is computed for Eastern Standard Time.

Gothic Tales

of H. P. Lovecraft

INSIGHT INTO the nature of the unseen world often comes from unlikely sources. Writers of Gothic and macabre tales, for instance, can create a feeling of the power of the transcendent almost in spite of themselves.

H.P. Lovecraft offers a prime example of this ability. A horror-story writer of the twenties and thirties, Lovecraft is preserved for our time through the advocacy of the late August Derleth and his publishing firm, Arkham House. *The Dunwich Horror and Other Stories* contains an excellent introduction to his work by Derleth and is available in a Lancer paperback. *The Tomb and Other Tales* (Bragle Books) is also an indispensable member of the Lovecraft canon.

Lovecraft, of course, followed a tradition in which truth was unimportant. His goal was to fascinate and terrify the reader and leave him with a shivery fear of dark corners and old places. Toward this end he invented a pantheon of primal incorporeal entities with names like Azathoth and Hastur who wait malevolently for a chance to visit unspeakable horror on the world.

Such work may be viewed as harmful to the followers of Wicca, for it fosters fear and hostility toward forces we believe are neither good nor evil but are simply there. Yet the power with which Lovecraft invokes a realm of existence beyond the one we see and touch testifies to its existence. Reading him, we experience a source of knowledge beyond the senses. We don't *learn about* this realm but *recognize* it, even though it is grossly distorted. Any sensitive reader of *The Dunwich Horror*, or *The Haunter of the Dark*, for example, will experience this insight, though we must disregard the implacable enmity toward our world with which Lovecraft endows his beings.

Through the ages storytellers and writers have used their fancies to entertain their audiences. Skillful ones like H.P. Lovecraft plumbed their souls to strike universal chords that resonate in those attuned to them. Adept readers can divine much about these chords through their work.

– Originally published in the 1972/1973 Witches' Almanac.

capricorn
December 21, 2014 – January 19, 2015
Cardinal Sign of Earth ♁ Ruled by Saturn ♄

S	M	T	W	T	F	S
Dec. 21 ● Capricorn	22 ⇐Winter Solstice ❄	23 WAXING	24 Kiss under mistletoe Aquarius	25	26 Hold a ghost's hand Pisces	27 Louis Pasteur born 1822
28 ◐ Aries	29	30 Make an earth charm Taurus	31	Jan. 1 2015	2 Feed the birds Gemini	3
4 ○ Wolf Moon Cancer	5 WANING	6 Abandon old habits Leo	7	8 Eat sunflower seeds	9 Feast of Janus Virgo	10
11 Libra	12 Snow!	13 ◐	14 Light a fire outdoors Scorpio	15	16 Slow down Sagittarius	17
18 John Partridge born 1644 Capricorn	19					

BETH (BIRCH)

Few trees figure more prominently in the folklore of Northern Europe than the birch. Deemed sacred to Thor, Norse god of thunder and lightning, the birch symbolizes youth and springtime. It is one of the hardiest trees in the world; growing further north, and, with the rowan and the ash, higher up mountains than any other species. The birch is called "the tree of inception" with good reason. Not only does it self-sow, forming groves, but it is one of the earliest forest trees to put out leaves in spring.
— excerpt from *Celtic Tree Magic*

Bellerophon and Pegasus, Gayley, 1893

aquarius

January 20 – February 18, 2015

Fixed Sign of Air ♎ Ruled by Uranus ♅

S	M	T	W	T	F	S
		Jan. 20 ● Aquarius	21 WAXING	22 Pisces	23	24 Aries
25	26 ◐ Taurus	27	28 *Jackson Pollock born 1912*	29 Gemini	30	31 *Gather falling snow* Cancer
Feb. 1 Oimelc Eve	2 Candlemas	3 ○ Storm Moon Leo	4 WANING	5 Virgo	6 *Visit a frozen pond*	7
8 Libra	9 *Talk with a friend*	10 Scorpio	11 ◐	12 Sagittarius	13	14 *Magic Sam born 1937*
15 Lupercalia Capricorn	16 *Cast a spell*	17	18 ● Aquarius			

LUIS (ROWAN)

Rowan figures prominently in Scottish folklore as a sure means to counteract evil intent. It was believed that a christened person need only touch a suspected witch with rowan wood in order to break a spell as the poet Alan Ramsay wrote: "Rowan tree and red thread, will put witches to their speed." Yet, a century earlier, in the case of Margaret Barclay, such a charm was damning evidence. Brought to trial for witchcraft in the town of Irvine, Ayrshire, Scotland in 1618, her conviction was assured when a piece of rowan tied with red yarn was found in her possession. *– excerpt from Celtic Tree Magic*

Perhaps they are not stars, but rather openings in heaven, where the love of our lost ones pours through and shines down upon us to let us know they are happy. — ESKIMO PROVERB

S	M	T	W	T	F	S
NION (ash) The Greeks dedicated the ash tree to Poseidon, god of the sea, and sailors carried its wood as protection against the threat of drowning. The major *(continued below)*				Feb. **19** Year of the Sheep WAXING Pisces	**20**	**21** Aries
22	**23** Taurus	**24**	**25** ◑ Gemini	**26**	**27** *Love with passion*	**28** *Zero Mostel born 1915* Cancer
March **1** Matronalia	**2** *Shed a tear* Leo	**3**	**4** *Look for the moon's ring* Virgo	**5** Chaste Moon	**6** WANING	**7** Libra
8	**9** *Mircea Eliade born 1907* Scorpio	**10**	**11** *Read a book*	**12** Sagittarius	**13** ◐	**14** Capricorn
15 *Daylight Savings Time begins @ 2am*	**16** Aquarius	**17**	**18** *Minerva's Day* ⇨ Pisces	**19** Total solar eclipse ⇨	**20** ●	

spiritual significance of the ash tree comes from Northern Europe, where as Yggdrasil, the World Tree, it connects the underworld, earth and heaven. The ash is associated in Norse myths with Odin (Woden), supreme among gods, who sought to increase his wisdom with extreme suffering. It was on an ash tree that he hanged himself.

– excerpt from *Celtic Tree Magic*

Cardinals

Sacred Sun Birds

SOARING HIGH above Earth toward the heavens, birds have been seen as celestial messengers and emblems of magic since earliest times. The lore of the feathered ones includes the mythological phoenix, reputed to rise to new life from the flames; the wise owl carried by both Minerva and Odin; heroic messenger pigeons entrusted with vital missives; and sinister crows.

The beautiful red cardinal is especially loved and admired. In recent years, cardinals have become increasingly popular choices for holiday greeting cards, as well as home décor and wardrobe accents. Folklore dictates that if a cardinal flies toward you it brings great good luck. Named for the bright red clerical robes worn by the cardinals of the Roman Catholic Church, this small and timid bird's message is consistently one of spirituality and happiness.

Cardinals have been selected seven times to be an official US state bird — more often than any other bird. They are found in the warmer regions of the Eastern USA, as well as in Mexico. Native American traditions dedicate cardinals to the sun and link them to sacred fires. Those fortunate enough to find a cardinal's fallen feather would do well to cherish it as a talisman. It augurs a turn of fortune for the better.

A Cherokee Legend

This tells of how Cardinal earned his beautiful red feathers. When the world was young, Raccoon played a trick on Wolf. As Wolf slept, Raccoon stopped his eyes shut with river clay. When Wolf awoke in distress, Cardinal took pity on him and pecked the clay from his eyes very carefully. The grateful Wolf showed Cardinal a magical pool where the water turned everything a beautiful red. The male cardinal dove in and turned a beautiful scarlet. Only a little bit of color remained by the time his mate arrived. She swam and swam, but still was left with just a hint of the red.

– MARINA BRYONY

aries

March 20 – April 19, 2015

Cardinal Sign of Fire △ Ruled by Mars ♂

S	M	T	W	T	F	S
ÞESTIA *Hestia, you who tend the holy house of the lord Apollo, the Far-shooter at goodly Pytho, with soft oil dripping ever from your locks, come now into this house, come, having one mind with Zeus the all-wise: draw near, and withal bestow grace upon my song. Hestia, in the* (continued below)					MAR. **20** 2015 Vernal Equinox	**21** Aries
22	**23** *Bless seeds* Taurus	**24**	**25** *Burn sage and cedar* Gemini	**26**	**27** 🌗 Cancer	**28**
29 *Pray to Apollo* Leo	**30** *Hellmut Wolff born 1906*	**31** *Make a mask*	APRIL **1** *All Fools' Day* Virgo	**2** *Plant first seeds*	**3** *Total lunar eclipse* ⇨ Libra	**4** 🌕 *Seed Moon*
5 WANING	**6** *Stanislaus Guaita born 1861* Scorpio	**7**	**8** *Enchant a fire* Sagittarius	**9**	**10**	**11** 🌓 Capricorn
12	**13** *Do not engage* Aquarius	**14** *Feel peace*	**15** Pisces	**16** *Bury evil*	**17** Aries	**18** 🌑
19 WAXING Taurus	♈	*high dwellings of all, both deathless gods and men who walk on earth, you have gained an everlasting abode and highest honour: glorious is your portion and your right. For without you mortals hold no banquet, — where one does not duly pour sweet wine in offering to Hestia both first and last.* — excerpt from *Homeric Hymns*				

55

The Field Mouse
& the House Mouse

ONCE a field mouse invited his friend the house mouse to dinner. Not satisfied with the meal of barley and wheat, the house mouse said to the field mouse, "There are so many good things to eat where I live! Come visit me and you'll taste a little of everything." So the two of them went to the house mouse's house, where they found vegetables, fruits, dates, honey and cheese. When the field mouse saw all this, he began to think that the house mouse's life was really much better than his own. But each time they were ready to begin eating, some man would suddenly open the door, and the poor mice would have to jump into a crack in the floor. Finally the field mouse, who was good and hungry by this time, said, "Friend, stay here and eat to your heart's content — if you don't mind all the trouble and the danger. I'll stick to my wheat and barley, as long as I can live in peace and quiet."

Moral: A simple life without worries is better than a rich life full of cares.

taurus

April 20 – May 20, 2015

Fixed Sign of Earth ♉ Ruled by Venus ♀

S	M	T	W	T	F	S
	APRIL 20 George Takei born 1937	21 Gemini	22 Earth Day	23 Cancer	24 Post a letter of love	25 Leo
26	27	28 Virgo	29 Honor Hawthorn spirits	30 Walpurgis Night	MAY 1 Beltane Libra	2
3 Hare Moon Scorpio	4 WANING	5 Sagittarius	6 Sing with the birds	7	8 White Lotus Day Capricorn	9
10 Friedrich Marby born 1882 Aquarius	11	12 Pisces	13	14 Wear red Aries	15	16 Bind an enemy Taurus
17	18 Gemini	19 WAXING	20 Cancer			

the khalkotauroi

He [Hephaistos] had also made him [Aeetes king of Kolkhis] Bulls with feet of bronze and bronze mouths from which the breath came out in flame, blazing and terrible. And he had forged a plough of indurated steel, all in one piece. All as a thank-offering to Helios, who had taken him up in his chariot when he sank exhausted on the battlefield of Phlegra. – excerpt from *Argonautica* (Greek epic 3rd BCE,)

PICKING THINGS UP:

Pins and pennies

See a penny and pick it up,
all the day you'll have good luck.
See a penny and let it lay,
bad luck you'll have all the day.
— Traditional rhyme

THE EARLIER VERSIONS of this popular nursery rhyme referred to pins, also called common pins, which are no longer very common, unless you sew or craft. They were made entirely of plain metal — no pretty glass heads — and were quite expensive. So expensive, in fact, that a "paper of pins" (a strip of paper pierced with pins) would be given as a gift. Women would allot a portion of the household budget to pins, necessary in making clothes. This practice gave rise to the phrase "pin money" and eventually covered not just money for items used in making clothes, but clothing itself, and eventually expanded to mean any money set aside for incidentals.

Finding an expensive item like a straight pin would be lucky in itself and even a sign that the gods were favoring you. To ignore a gift from the gods —  some believed that all metal was a gift from the gods — would be an insult, bringing down their wrath in the form of bad luck.

The position of the pin, when found, has significance. If the point is toward you, it can bring good luck, but only if you then either stick it in a piece of wood or pin it in your coat with the point toward the back. If you come upon it with the head facing you, a message awaits. If you find it crossing your way — that is, lying with its side toward you — then you will see your love that day.

The rhyme has evolved to use the word penny instead of pin, which still fits with the idea that finding a thing of value is good luck. A penny, like a pin, is also metal, signifying a gift from the gods. In 1793, the young United States of America began minting copper pennies. The British followed in 1797. Copper is ruled by Venus, which leads some to believe that the luck that comes with picking up copper is not financial, but related to love.

Once again, some say that the lie of the penny, when found, has an influence on whether the luck will be good or bad. A penny found heads up is always considered good luck, but a penny found head down is not. I always pick up pennies, even those laying tails up. To ward off any bad luck, I simply say this charm as I pick it up: "As I do will, so mote it be, any penny is lucky for me."

– MORVEN WESTFIELD

gemini

May 21 – June 20, 2015

Mutable Sign of Air ♎ Ruled by Mercury ☿

S	M	T	W	T	F	S
phoenix Most creatures spring from other creatures. But there is only one phoenix ranging the sky, and this rarest of birds clones itself (continued below)				MAY **21** *Carry two seeds for luck*	**22**	**23** Leo
24	**25** Virgo	**26**	**27** *Marie Anne Lenormand born 1772* Libra	**28**	**29** Oak Apple Day	**30** Scorpio
31 *Watch witches fly*	JUNE **1** Vesak Day	**2** Dyad Moon Sagittarius	**3** WANING	**4** *Read dice* Capricorn	**5** Night of the Watchers	**6** Aquarius
7 *Walk a path*	**8** Pisces	**9**	**10** *Meditate on temperance* Aries	**11**	**12** *Eat an apple* Taurus	**13**
14	**15** *The winds bring messages* Gemini	**16**	**17** WAXING Cancer	**18** *Roger Ebert born 1946* Leo	**19**	**20**

everlastingly from the burned bones of its own body... early alchemists were located by the sign of the phoenix above the door. The Old Testament mentions the bird in Job, and Christian monks who wrote medieval bestiaries took the phoenix as a point of departure for a scolding: "If the Phoenix has the power to die and rise again, why, silly man, are you scandalized at the word of God."

– excerpt from *The Little Book of Magical Creatures*

Monday's child is fair of face,
Tuesday's child is full of grace;
Wednesday's child is full of woe,
Thursday's child has far to go;
Friday's child is loving and giving,
Saturday's child works hard for its living;
But the child that is born on the Sabbath day
Is bonny and blithe, and good and gay.

                – MOTHER GOOSE

cancer

June 21 – July 22, 2015

Cardinal Sign of Water ▽ Ruled by Moon ☽

S	M	T	W	T	F	S
June 21 Summer Solstice ☼	22 Gather Saint Johnswort Virgo	23 Midsummer ⇨	24 ◑ Libra	25 Anthony Bourdain born 1956	26 Touch agate	27 Scorpio
28	29 Wish upon the moon Sagittarius	30	July 1 ◔ Mead Moon Capricorn	2 WANING	3 Drink from a spring Aquarius	4
5 Avoid the rain Pisces	6	7	8 ◐ Aries	9	10 Be proud Taurus	11
12 Gemini	13 Arthur Dee born 1579	14 Gather sea water Cancer	15 ●	16 WAXING	17 Spend time with familiars Leo	18
19 Virgo	20	21	22 Libra			

DRAGONS

The Oriental dragon has always been a benevolent beast. Visual conceptions vary. The Chinese and Japanese dragons are scaly serpents, while the European equivalent is lizardlike and winged. Despite the difference in appearance and aspect, dragons universally share an association with water, caves, and hidden places where treasure is concealed. Guarding secret wealth is the function most often performed by the dragon in legends and myths from all over the world.

– excerpt from *Witches All*

☉ The Magic Square of the Sun ☉

6	32	3	34	35	1
7	11	27	28	8	30
19	14	16	15	23	24
18	20	22	21	17	13
25	29	10	9	26	12
36	5	33	4	2	31

A MAGIC SQUARE is a matrix that focuses the spiritual force of a planet in a mathematical fashion. Each one of the seven ancient planets has its own square that can be used as a talisman for creating the change that is needed at any given time.

The Magic Square should be made on the day and hour of the planet that you are working with and the ink should be the color attributed to the planet. One should begin with a blank grid with the required number of rows and columns. Lastly, when drawing the Magic Square, the numbers should be placed in sequence, beginning with the number one.

The Magic Square of the Sun can be used to transform any situation from one of impotence to virility. The Sun is said to bring on an atmosphere where you can become renowned, amiable, and acceptable. In fact, using the Sun's Magic Square will create a potency in all works and success in all endeavors. When using the Sun's Magic Square you should be careful that its influence does not cause you to become a tyrant, overly proud or ambitious and impossible to satisfy.

Work with the Sun's Magic Square should be done on a Sunday. To find out the hour of the Sun, divide the daylight hours into twelve equal parts. The first "hour" of sunlight on a Sunday is the hour of the Sun. If you are going to work in the evening, the same process is done: divide the nighttime hours by twelve. The third hour is the "hour" of the Sun. The color associated with the Sun is gold or yellow, so your square should be done in those colors.

Good luck and may your magic be successful!

– DEVON STRONG

leo

July 23 – August 22, 2015
Fixed Sign of Fire △ Ruled by Sun ☉

LEO

S	M	T	W	T	F	S
LION *Its mane like tongues of fire, the golden lion is traditionally a beast of the sun. Probably because of its strength and size it was from* (continued below)				JULY **23** Ancient Egyptian New Year	**24** Scorpio	**25** Chant "ISA"
26 Sagittarius	**27** Norman Lear born 1922	**28**	**29** Bake bread Capricorn	**30** Lughnassad Eve ⇨	**31** Wort Moon Aquarius	AUGUST **1** Lammas 🌿
2 WANING Pisces	**3** Create a puddle	**4** Light a candle Aries	**5**	**6** Taurus	**7**	**8** Feed the birds Gemini
9	**10** Read the Tarot Cancer	**11**	**12** Eat walnuts	**13** Diana's Day Leo	**14**	**15** WAXING Virgo
16 Eydie Gorme born 1928	**17** Black Cat Appreciation day	**18** Help a friend Libra	**19**	**20** Scorpio	**21** Read a book	**22**

earliest times associated with deities and royalty and as a symbolic guardian in stone still functions not only outside temples but libraries and palaces as well. "The lion stands on a hill," wrote the anonymous author of a thirteenth-century English bestiary. "If he hears a man hunting, or smells him through his nose, scenting his approach — by whatsoever way he wishes to go down into the valley, all his footprints he fills in after him.

— excerpt from *Witches All*

Here's to thee, Old Apple Tree

WASSAIL is known today in the U.S. as a hot cider drink, commonly consumed at the mid-winter holidays. But to the knowledgeable U.K. resident, it is a festive brew made from most any type of fruit. The earliest known apple wassailing — also known as 'apple howling'— was in Fordwich, Kent in approximately 1585.

Stories and songs surround the Wassailing tradition:

"Drink the drink and
make an offering to the tree,
Wassail brings luck and
bounty for thee."

Custom has it that songs regaling the power of the Wassailing be sung over future crops. The last drops of the old drink are poured upon the roots of the oldest or most prolific fruit-bearing trees to ensure a good crop for the next year.

There are a great many old familiar Wassail chants and rhymes. An early example:

"Here's to thee,
old apple-tree,
Whence thou may'st
bud, and Whence
thou may'st blow,
And whence thou
may'st bear
Apples enow!
Hats-full! Caps-full!
Bushel, bushel, sacks-full!
And my pockets full, too! Hurra!"

Recipes for the old-style drink vary greatly, depending on location and according to each old family recipe. You'll find our recipe for Wassail in Kitchen Magic on page 110.

virgo

August 23 – September 21, 2015

Mutable Sign of Earth ♍ Ruled by Mercury ☿

S	M	T	W	T	F	S
Aug. 23 Sagittarius	24	25 Geraldine Ferraro born 1935 Capricorn	26	27 Aquarius	28	29 Barley Moon Pisces
30 WANING	31 Aries	Sept. 1 Stay balanced	2 Make a poppet Taurus	3	4 Write down your dreams Gemini	5
6 Keep your promise	7 Cancer	8	9 Leo	10 Be humble	11 Don't be too serious Virgo	12 George Jones born 1931
13	14 Partial solar ⇐ eclipse Libra	15 WAXING	16 Avoid temptation	17 Ganesh Festival Scorpio	18	19 Dance! Sagittarius
20	21 Capricorn	22 Taste something sweet				

ASTRON

With holy voice I call the stars [Astron] on high, pure sacred lights and genii of the sky. Celestial stars, the progeny of Night [Nyx], in whirling circles beaming far your light. Refulgent rays around the heav'ns ye throw, eternal fires, the source of all below... In seven bright zones ye run with wand'ring flames, and heaven and earth compose your lucid frames: With course unwearied, pure and fiery bright forever shining thro' the veil of Night. Hail twinkling, joyful, ever wakeful fires!... These sacred rites regard with conscious rays, and end our works devoted to your praise.

– excerpt from *Orphic Hymn to the Stars*

holly

Tinne

SOME OCCULTISTS place yew as the eighth tree representing the consonants in the tree alphabet of the Druids. Others, however, call for holly to follow the oak. This sequence accords with many folktales and celebrations that present the oak and holly trees as two Divine Kings, one representing the waxing half of the year when the sun rises to its height at summer solstice, the other as symbol of the waning cycle as the sun retreats to its lowest point at midwinter solstice. The Celtic myth of Sir Gawain and the Green Knight has the two opponents meeting in combat at midsummer and midwinter. Gawain carries a club of oak. The Green Knight's weapon is a bough of holly.

Holly is an evergreen growing as an under-shrub in many woods and forests. Some varieties given space and opportunity will grow to be 40 feet tall. The waxy surface of its thick leaves enables the holly to resist water loss when the soil is frozen. The dark green lower leaves have sharp spines which discourage browsing animals during the winter months. The holly is either male or female and both bear flowers, but the female flowers develop into bright red berries in autumn. Country wisdom advises that one should always plant a pair of hollies to allow for cross-fertilization. A barren holly is regarded as unlucky.

The oak, ash and holly were favored trees in the sacred groves of the Druids. The holly had a strong association with divination in Northern Europe. A charm to bring a dream of your future mate required nine spiky leaves of holly collected at midnight before moonrise. Complete silence was to be observed as you wrapped the leaves in a square of pure white linen, placed the packet under your pillow and dreamed the night away.

The Romans decorated their homes with boughs of holly during the December festival of Saturnalia; Mediterranean "holly" comes from the evergreen kermes or holly oak with a leaf form identical to the true holly of the north. This tree, too, was credited with magical power. Pliny, in the first century CE, wrote, "A holly tree planted in a town house or a country house keeps off uncanny influences."

66

libra

September 22 – October 22, 2015

Cardinal Sign of Air ♎ *Ruled by Venus* ♀

LIBRA

S	M	T	W	T	F	S
			Sept. 23 Autumnal Equinox ♌	24 *Change your luck* Aquarius	25	26 *Shed no tears* Pisces
27 Blood Moon	28 WANING Total lunar ⇐ eclipse Aries	29 *Make corn dollies*	30 Taurus	Oct. 1 *Gather Fall's leaves*	2 Gemini	3 *Allan Kardec born 1804*
4 Cancer	5	6 *Harvest pumpkins* Leo	7	8	9 *Brew tea* Virgo	10
11 *Cleanse your home* Libra	12	13 WAXING	14 *Beware of monsters* Scorpio	15	16 Sagittarius	17 *Bestow an amulet*
18	19 *Thomas Browne born 1605* Capricorn	20	21 Aquarius	22 *Count coins*	**ʜepʜaɛsᴛus** Strong, mighty Hephaistos, bearing splendid light, unwearied fire, with flaming torrents bright: strong-	

handed, deathless, and of art divine, pure element, a portion of the world is thine: all-taming artist, all-diffusive power, 'tis thine, supreme, all substance to devour: aether, sun, moon, and stars, light pure and clear, for these thy lucid parts to men appear… Hear, blessed power, to holy rites incline, and all propitious on the incense shine: suppress the rage of fire's unwearied frame, and still preserve our nature's vital flame.

– excerpt from *Orphic Hymn to Hephaestus*

Service of the Dead

IF YOU ARE FOOLISH ENOUGH to watch by the gate of a church's graveyard at midnight on All Hallows Night, you may be sufficiently ill-fated to see the Service of the Dead — a most disturbing sight indeed. A vision of those who will die within the coming year marching before you might be alarming in and of itself, but there is always the chance that you are in danger of being the first-comer yourself. Should you be the unlucky one, you will become the Churchyard Walker and the Guardian of the Graveyard, until another foolhardy person disturbs the Service of the Dead on this most powerful night of the year. The person who is clandestinely touched by the Church-Yard Walker (the sight of him alone could cause one to perish of fright) dies on the spot.

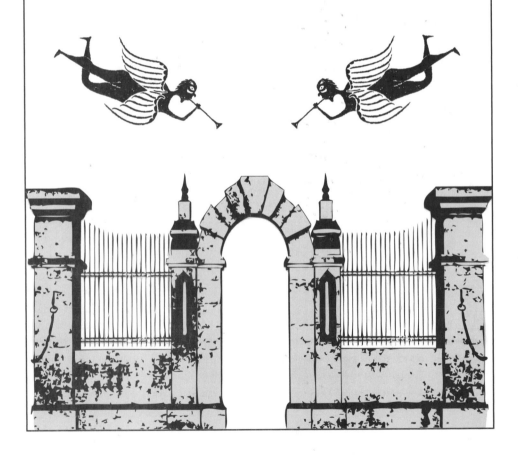

SCORPIVS

S	M	T	W	T	F	S
	PROMETHEUS *Prometheus, however, who was accustomed to scheming, planned by his own efforts to bring back the fire that had been taken from men. So,* (continued below) *the*				Oct. 23 Pisces	24 George Crumb born 1929
25 Aries	26	27 Snow Moon Taurus	28 WANING	29 Gather ancestor photos Gemini	30 Honor the dead	31 Samhain Eve Cancer
Nov. 1 Daylight Savings Time ends @ 2am	2 Hallowmas ⇦ Leo	3	4	5 Feed wild beasts Virgo	6	7
8 Patti Page born 1927 Libra	9	10 Gaze into the crystal Scorpio	11	12 WAXING Sagittarius	13 Cast a spell	14
15 Pray to the moon Capricorn	16 Hecate Night	17 Aquarius	18 Light white candles	19 Pisces	20	21 Cleanse the home Aries

others were away, he approached the fire of Jove, and with a small bit of this shut in a fennel-stalk he came joyfully, seeming to fly, not to run, tossing the stalk so that the air shut in with its vapours should not put out the flame in so narrow a space. Up to this time then, men who bring good news usually come with speed. In the rivalry of the games they also make it a practice for the runners to run, shaking torches after the manner of Prometheus. — excerpt from *Pseudo-Hyginus, Astronomica*

Notable Quotations

FIRE

Just as a candle cannot burn without fire, men cannot live without a spiritual life. — *Buddha*

"Torch is known to every living man by its flame, clear and bright; it burns oftenest where princes sit at ease indoors."
— *Anglo-Saxon Rune Poem*

It is with our passions as it is with fire and water; they are good servants, but bad masters.
— *Roger L'Estrange*

Fire is the most tolerable third party. — *Henry David Thoreau*

Playing with fire is bad for those who burn themselves. For the rest of us, it is a very great pleasure.
— *Author unknown*

A mighty flame followeth a tiny spark. — *Dante Alighieri*

For gold is tried in the fire and acceptable men in the furnace of adversity. — *George Santayana*

Fire is never a gentle master.
— *Proverb*

This is the truth: as from a fire aflame thousands of sparks come forth, even so from the Creator an infinity of beings have life and to him return again.
— *Marcus Tullius Cicero*

The flames of you the mighty are spread wide around: your splendour reaches to the sky. The gods enkindle you their ancient messenger. — *Rig Veda: Hymn to Agni, God of Fire*

Quotes compiled by Isabel Kunkle.

sagittarius

November 22 – December 20, 2015

Mutable Sign of Fire △ Ruled by Jupiter ♃

S	M	T	W	T	F	S
Nov. 22	23 Paint rune stones Taurus	24	25 Oak Moon	26 WANING Gemini	27	28 Encourage laughter Cancer
29	30 Winston Churchill born 1874 Leo	Dec. 1 Decorate for the season	2 Virgo	3	4 Listen to your heart	5 Libra
6 Gather with friends	7	8 Snow falls Scorpio	9	10 Foretell the future Sagittarius	11	12 WAXING Capricorn
13 Hang mistletoe	14 Aquarius	15 Tim Conway born 1933	16 Fairy Queen Eve	17 Prepare for the feast Saturnalia Pisces	18	19 Aries

20 helios

Golden Titan [Helios the Sun], whose eternal eye with matchless sight illumines all the sky. Native, unwearied in diffusing light, and to all eyes the object of delight: Lord of the seasons, beaming light from far, sonorous, dancing in thy four-yoked car. With thy right hand the source of morning light, and with thy left the father of the night. Agile and vigorous, venerable Sun, fiery and bright around the heavens you run . . . borne by lucid steeds . . . Bright eye, that round the world incessant flies, doomed with fair fulgid rays to set and rise . . . of steeds the ruler, and of life the light: with sounding whip four fiery steeds you guide, when in the glittering car of day you ride.

– excerpt from *Orphic Hymn to Helios*

TAROT'S DEVIL

THE DEVIL.

THE DEVIL perches on harpy's feet upon a stone altar, his sycophants chained at his feet. His crown is an inverted pentagram sat firmly between ram's horns; his bat's wings spread out menacingly behind him. His form, represented by the fifteenth card of the Major Arcana, is the demonic inverse of the angelic figure depicted on the sixth card of the Major Arcana. In fact, a closer look reveals his supplicants to be The Lovers, metamorphosed into beasts through their contact with the sensual world. At first, their submission and transformation is terrifying, an expression of a complete loss of self. But The Devil only offers pleasures of the flesh; the seeker must choose to indulge. The chains around their neck are loose and could be easily slipped, yet they remain. They choose to stay. The Devil welcomes all those driven from the garden with open arms.

The Devil represents the material world. Desires for money, power and pleasure are all governed by him and can easily corrupt the spirit of weaker individuals. However, contact with the material world is still vital for spiritual growth. It is The Devil who implores you to stop and smell the roses.

The Devil is temptation incarnate; his presence reminding us we need not be chained to our desires — our impulses towards sex, food, drink and other expressions of hedonistic abandon — but we need not cower in fear of them either.

capricorn
December 21, 2015 – January 19, 2016
Cardinal Sign of Earth ♀ Ruled by Saturn ♄

S	M	T	W	T	F	S
	DEC. 21 Winter Solstice ❄ Taurus	22	23 Gemini	24 Howl at the moon	25 Wolf Moon Cancer	26 WANING
27 Watch the sun rise Leo	28	29 Rescue a pet	30 Austin Osman Spare born 1886 Virgo	31	JAN. 1 2016 Libra	2
3	4 Make a poppet Scorpio	5	6 Bonnie Franklin born 1944 Sagittarius	7 The Fates know	8 Feast of Janus ⇨ Capricorn	9
10 WAXING	11 Enjoy fine music Aquarius	12	13 Heal the sick Pisces	14	15 Beware of flames Aries	16
17 Taurus	18 Guard your treasures	19 Gemini				

SALAMANDER

The zoological salamander is an unremarkable little amphibian that resembles a lizard. But its mythological counter-part has a uniquely wondrous quality — a body so icy that it can withstand flames. Belief concerning the salamander's marvelous virtue existed in ancient Egypt and Babylon. In Greece, Aristotle wrote that the salamander "not only walks through fire, but puts it out in doing so."... A medieval monk kept the myth alive by recording: "This animal is the only one which puts the flames out. Indeed, it lives in the middle of the blaze without being hurt and without being burnt."

– excerpt from *The Little Book of Magical Creatures*

YEAR OF THE WOOD SHEEP
February 19, 2015 – February 7, 2016

Chinese New Year is celebrated at the second New Moon after the Winter Solstice, in late January to mid-February. The Chinese calendar, based on a twelve year cycle, has been in use since at least 2637 BCE and is the oldest of all contemporary calendars.

An intriguing legend describes the origin of Chinese astrology. Twelve animals attended a party honoring Buddha. Each was rewarded with a year. These animals are said to hide in the hearts of those born, as well as within events that occur, during their respective years. Five elements (fire, water, metal, earth, and wood) characterize this zodiac. Every sixty years, the element and animal pairs return to begin a new cycle.

The sheep (a.k.a. the goat) was the eighth animal to arrive at the party. In the Far East, the number eight is considered especially auspicious, so the year holds promise of greater peace and prosperity for many. Lambs and goats symbolize sacrifice and spirituality: this sign accents faith. Religious practices become a stronger focus and a more universal source of solace.

Considered witty, loyal, altruistic, compliant, candid, kindly, tolerant, and mild mannered, Sheep people are sought after as business and marriage partners. The wood element also promises especially high intelligence, talent, and a gift for communicating with those from all walks of life. The Wood Sheep fares well in business, but is also a mystic, often revealing genuine psychic ability.

If you are a Sheep, prepare to move ahead and graze happily in greener pastures. Prospects will improve during your year.

Years of the Sheep

1931, 1943, 1955, 1967, 1979, 1991, 2003, 2015

More information on the Wood Sheep can be found on our website at http://The WitchesAlmanac.com/AlmanacExtras/.

Illustration by Ogmios MacMerlin

aquarius

January 20 – February 18, 2016

Fixed Sign of Air △ Ruled by Uranus ♅

S	M	T	W	T	F	S
hawk *Early Egyptians, observing the bird's dominion of the airy realm, referred to it as "God of the Sky." They named the* (continued below)			Jan. 20	21 Gregori Rasputin born 1869 Cancer	22	23 Storm Moon
24 WANING Leo	25	26 Mind your health Virgo	27	28 Libra	29 Gather with friends	30
31 Scorpio	Feb. 1 Oimelc Eve	2 Candlemas Sagittarius	3 Focus your mind	4	5 Capricorn	6 Adam Weishaupt born 1748
7 Year of the Monkey ⇨ Aquarius	8	9 WAXING Pisces	10	11 Exercise caution Aries	12 Dine with your beloved	13 Taurus
14 Lupercalia ⇨	15 Gemini	16 Show compassion	17	18 Cancer		

hawk Horus and worshipped him before the dynasties began, believing that this bird's quality defined a vision of all that was worthy of respect and devotion. His right eye represented the Sun; his left, the Moon; the stars shone in his speckled plumage. Temple priests must have tamed and tended the wild birds, for they were depicted in ancient art perched on a block without tether, free to fly as they chose. – excerpt from *The Little Book of Magical Creatures*

75

If they would eat nettles in March
And mugwort in May
So many young maidens
Would not turn to clay.

– ANONYMOUS
AND CENTURIES OLD

pisces

February 19 – March 20, 2016

Mutable Sign of Water ▽ Ruled by Neptune ♆

PISCES

S	M	T	W	T	F	S
		CHIMERA Chimera is another Greek mythological animal you don't want to chance meeting, not even in your *(continued below)*			FEB. **19**	**20** Leo
21	**22** Chaste Moon — Virgo	**23** WANING	**24** *Giovanni Mirandola born 1463*	**25** Libra	**26** *A new birth*	**27** Scorpio
28 *Gamble just a little*	**29** *Leap Year Day*	MARCH **1** Sagittarius	**2** *Matronalia* ⇦	**3** Capricorn	**4** *Play games of chance*	**5** Aquarius
6	**7** *Total solar eclipse* ⇨	**8** Pisces	**9** WAXING	**10** *Start a new project* Aries	**11**	**12** Taurus
13 *Robert Felkin born 1853*	**14** Gemini	**15**	**16** Cancer	**17** *Hold tight*	**18** Leo	**19** *Minerva's Day*
20 *Daylight Savings Time begins @ 2am*	dreams. The beast would be easy enough to recognize, having the head of a lion, the torso of a goat, and the tail of a serpent… the chimera has a fiery breath that sizzles to a crisp anything within range except the odd hero. Homer tells us that "Her pitchy nostrils flaky flames expire; / Her gaping throat emits infernal fire." – excerpt from *The Little Book of Magical Creatures*					

The Return of the Sun

Winter festivals in fire and ice

WHILE Father Time limps away as December 31 nears and Baby New Year waits to follow him at midnight on January 1, the sensitive issues of inevitable death making way for birth and new beginnings are welcomed in the various symbols linked to the winter holidays. From Yule logs to candles and Christmas tree lights, fires are kindled in different ways to brighten and warm the cold stillness during the winter holidays. There is Christmas for Christians, Diwali for Hindus, and Hanukkah for Jews. The secular celebrations of Kwanzaa for African Americans and Festivas (originally for Seinfeld fans, but recently adopted by atheists) round out the merriment. The cyclical rebirth of the sun (Son), the spirit of life, is honored near the winter solstice, the time when the dark days gradually begin to lengthen.

Wiccans celebrate deep winter near December 21 with Yuletide. The word "Yule" may derive from an Anglo-Saxon term for "wheel." The winter holiday season references a cycle or seasonal circle, which has been spinning from some starting point too long in the past to date. Wreaths are a familiar and beloved form of winter holiday décor. These unbroken circles of evergreen branches, often decorated with red ribbons, illustrate the idea of everlasting eternal life. The seasonal colors of red and green hint at the mixture of animal (red) and plant (green) energies dwelling within each of us. The vivid contrast of these colors, which oppose each other on the color wheel, show the contrasts and extremes struggling for balance and control within human nature.

The 14th century Arthurian legend, *Sir Gawain and the Green Knight* begins at a winter holiday festival in King Arthur's court and culminates at the summer solstice six months later. This tale is a really splendid illustration of the polarities of red and green. Since Plato's time, philosophers have taught that we are partly ethereal (mind) and part animal (body). The winter holiday season offers joyful and poignant reminders of this.

Fragrances and Plants

There are magical plants and fragrances linked to Yule. Pine, because of its shape and evergreen needles, suggests the flame of eternal life. The Christmas or Yule tree, decorated with lights and ornaments, reflects legends of sacred trees from Scandinavian, Hebrew, and Biblical texts, as well as other traditions. Think of the Nordic *Ygdrassil*, the Tree of Life in the Kabbalah, and so forth.

Holly, cedar, and juniper also are sacred to the promise of eternity, by virtue of their perpetual greenery. A crown worn by the Holly King, a spirit of the season who is prominent in festivals at Yuletide and in early legends, illustrates this. Many historians consider Glastonbury in Great Britain to have been the site of Camelot. The name Glastonbury suggests the Irish and Cornish words for holly. Holly's lyrical partner, ivy, was once brewed into potent winter ale. The wood of the ivy was carved to make goblets and the leaves were chewed to enhance the euphoria. Ivy was among the first popular house plants. Its mere presence projects an aura of hospitality and friendship.

The beloved holiday mistletoe is among the most mysterious, magical, and sacred of plants. Mistletoe reflects the earthier magic of the winter holidays. Its name means "sacred tree" in Old Norse. Mistletoe offers the power of life and fertility, as evidenced by the white berries. Since earliest times it has been called a bestower of health, a protector of love, and generator of passion. Leadership, invulnerability and protection from storms are also among mistletoe's many attributes. In medieval times it was forbidden to fight in the presence of mistletoe, so it's a symbol of peace.

Tradition tells us that mistletoe must be plucked without a blade and never allowed to touch the ground to preserve its powers. Hang the fresh mistletoe leaves high in the home at Yuletide. The leaves can be gathered into a bit of cloth, which is then tied with yarn or ribbon. Leave it there for an entire year, and then toss it on the hearth fire at the year's end, while giving thanks. Replace the discarded leaves with a fresh bundle of mistletoe at once. Lingering beneath the mistletoe for an excuse to exchange holiday kisses has remained standard in holiday revelry throughout the ages. To add sparkle to your relationship, give it a try!

Bayberry Candles

The bayberry candle, if lit between December 21st and Twelfth Night (January 6) carries one of the loveliest of all holiday legends. The waxy outer covering of the bayberry is fragrant, burns well, and is associated with Jupiter, the planet of wealth and health. An old rhyme reads:

> *Bayberry candles*
> *burned to the socket,*
> *bring health, love and gold*
> *in the pocket!*

True bayberry wax is a soft bluish grey-green color, but it can be dyed red or bright green. By the light of a bayberry candle, bind a bundle of the sacred plants, which most attract you with red ribbon. Keep it as a charm to guard the dark nights.

– GRANIA LING

Walpurgisnacht

ACCORDING to German folk legend, on Walpurgisnacht (May Eve), witches gathered from the four corners of the world to attend the Witches' Sabbat. Riding brooms and goats, they flew to a mist-shrouded mountain peak called the Brocken or Blocksberg.

A 1732 hand-drawn map with the caption *Darstellung des Brockens* (Representation of the Brocken) shows at least six witches in the air and two men dancing at the top of the mountain.

Legends of Devil Worship

The witches in the legend were often portrayed as minions of the devil. A wood carving by Johannes Praetorius in 1668 depicts the witches showing their devotion to the devil. In the carving we see a follower ritually kissing the devil on the buttocks. This act, called the Kiss of Shame or the Kiss of Infamy (*osculum infame*), was alleged to be an act of greeting. In the foreground we see a devil appearing to defecate into a large pot. To

his right, a woman has been seized by another devil, his muscular arm holding her to him. Above and to the left of them, we see another devil groping at a naked woman.

Johann Wolfgang von Goethe also seized upon the devil theme in his drama *Faust*. The title character Faust has sold his soul to Mephistopheles, the devil, signing a contract with his own blood. Together they ascend the Brocken.

Stoker and Black Sabbath

"Dracula's Guest," a short story by Bram Stoker that was originally part of the novel *Dracula*, but cut from the novel for length, shows knowledge of the Walpurgisnacht legends. The main character is traveling in Germany. As the coach is about to the leave the hotel, the maitre d' warns the coachman to be back by nightfall, due to the weather, but adds that he is sure that the coachman will not be late, "For you know what night it is." When the guest asks the coachman what night it is, the coachman crosses himself as he answers, "Walpurgisnacht."

Another woodcut of a witch giving a ritual kiss to Satan. From R.P. Gauccius' Compendium Maleficarum, *Milan, 1626*

Later, after dark clouds blot the sky, the horses become unreasonably unquiet, and the coachman leaves in fear, Stoker remarks: "Walpurgis Night, when, according to the belief of millions of people, the devil was abroad — when the graves were opened and the dead came forth and walked. When all evil things of earth and air and water held revel."

A more-recent reference to the alleged evil of Walpurgisnacht is in the song "Walpurgis" by Black Sabbath, which starts with the line "Witches gather at black masses." (Later the song's title would change to "War Pigs" and the first line would start "Generals gathered in their masses.")

But, as often is the case, all of these legends were laid over earlier Pagan legends that told a different story. Instead of demons and devils cavorting in the open air, earlier tales told of

believers gathering on the Broken to celebrate the wedding of Odin to Freya or to perform rituals to chase away the darkness of winter. Above the tree line, the peak is often covered in snow from September to May. Surely it needed some help in banishing winter!

The Witches' Dance Floor

The *Hexentanzplatz* (literally "Witches' Dance Floor") is another Harz mountain site associated with devilish witches that is also believed to have been a pre-Christian site of worship. A plateau 454 m above sea level, it is not quite as high as the Brocken (just under 1142 m), and lacks the eerie atmosphere of its higher, foggier cousin. May Eve festivals were held on the Hexentanzplatz in honor of the forest and mountain goddesses. One tradition has it that the Hexentanzplatz got its reputation for devilry when the Pagan practices were banned by invading Christian Franks. To protect their fellow worshippers from the guards stationed there on May Eve, some dressed up as evil witches to scare the guards away.

The new religion of Christianity had another effect on the area. May Eve was renamed after a Christian saint, Saint Walburga or Walpurga, giving us Walpurgisnacht ("Walpurga's night").

The Brocken Today

The Brocken is now part of the Harz National Park. The signs there allude to the devilry legend, with a logo of a devil (*teufel*) in profile. This image conforms to the typical devil Halloween costume: horns, beaked nose, sharp chin (or beard?), pitchfork, pointy tail, and what could be cloven hooves.

A modern sign at the Brocken

The witch logo is also shown in profile. Flying astride a broom, the witch wears a kerchief instead of the wide-brimmed conical hat we see in cartoon images of the witch in the United States. An old souvenir plate from the Harz, now exhibited at the Witches' Museum in Boscastle, Cornwall, United Kingdom, also shows a kerchiefed hag astride a broom as she rides over the countryside.

One reaches the Brocken via the narrow-gauge Brocken Railway on a charming old steam train. Built in the late 1890s, this railway sustained significant damage to the track during the second World War, but continued to operate. When the Berlin Wall went up on August 13, 1961, the station was no longer accessible to the public: the Brocken was inhabited by East German border troops and Soviet soldiers. After German reunification, it wasn't clear if the railway would continue to operate. We have the united efforts of railway enthusiasts to thank for its continuation. After renovation (and removal of military items), the railway reopened to the public on September 15, 1991.

The Brocken Specter

The weather is responsible for something known as the Brocken specter, where a visitor's shadow creates strange optical effects when it falls upon the fog. The fog helps the summit retain the charm of a wild and mysterious place, despite the large television tower originally built in 1935 and rebuilt in 1947. An industrial-looking building houses a modern museum.

Unfortunately, the signs and placards in the museum are only in German, but by picking out some of the words that are similar to English — and by copying down the text for later translation — you can tell that the exhibit talks less of devil worship and more of nature-worshipping Pagans who believed that the land and plants contained spirits and who used herbs, berries, and roots for healing.

Servants of the Devil

The signs explain that women who had medical skills were often considered witches and in the Middle Ages that meant that they were perceived as servants of the devil. One sign suggested that the inhospitable climate of the Brocken and its inaccessibility played strongly on the imagination of the people. The first recorded ascent of the mountain wasn't until 1572. If there were truly meetings of devil-worshipping witches, they would have been able to conduct their meetings without a thought about interference. And likewise, if instead there were nature-worshipping Pagans conducting rituals to scare away the devils, no one would see that.

The train to the top is expensive (32 Euro at the time of this writing) and some of the comments on a travel review site suggest that the train and site are not fully wheelchair-accessible. There are no snacks or water on the train. If you're interested in visiting this wild and eerie site, avoid the month of August (crowded) and do your research before you go. The small town of Wernigerode and the Brocken are not heavily traveled by English-speaking tourists, but a good guidebook with German phrases should get you through.

Hexentanzplatz Today

Whereas the Brocken is a wild and eerie place, the Hexentanzplatz is often compared to a theme park aimed at families. A gondola-lift runs from the town of Thale to the Hexentanzplatz where there is a small museum explaining the Witches' Sabbath, a zoo, and a tourist center.

Three ghoulish bronze sculptures were added to the site in 1996. The devil is shown sitting on a boulder with his legs widely apart, showing his naked genitals. A witch, also naked, pushes a large boulder. On a third boulder sits the devil's "assistant," a creature who is part pig, rodent, and dragon.

Hexentanzplatz is a popular place for Germans to celebrate their version of Halloween. Every year from April 30 to May 1, the celebration of Walpurgisnacht draws thousands of visitors, many dressing as cartoonish witches or devils. On this night, the attendants are definitely adult, in contrast to the family aspect at other times of the day or year. Beer flows and bonfires are lit. After midnight, an actor in the guise of the devil gives a speech to the crowd and selects a May Queen. In other words, visiting the Hexentanzplatz on May Eve is like visiting Salem, Massachusetts on Halloween: a lot of fun, but not a quiet religious experience.

– MORVEN WESTFIELD

More photos of The Brocken can be found at www.TheWitchesAlmanac.com/AlmanacExtras.

Window on the Weather

The natural variance of our planet's seasonal cycles continues to mystify, as ancient established variances begin anew. Solar radiance plays a continued pivotal role, regulating Earth's temperature variances and bringing seasonal surprises to some. While the Northern Hemisphere's eastern domains have encountered brief summers and icy winter air, the west is parched and in need of replenishing rains born of Pacific storms. The storms have been lacking, though more recently the emergence of El Niño brings hope that recent drought conditions will be eased. Furthermore, relative calm in the Atlantic Ocean may continue so long as the same pattern that brings drought relief to the west remains in effect. Winters are likely to remain snowy and cold east of the Rockies for some time as Arctic Sea ice continues its slow recovery. Rainfall may remain sparse in the west for some time, a challenge for farmers. Analogue long range forecasting with the sun as a driving force is the domain of this year's Window on the Weather.

– TOM C. LANG

SPRING

MARCH 2015. Volatile and harsh winter cold slowly eases this week. Even the coldest days early in the month are disguised by the return of the sun. Still, with lingering Arctic air, contrasting temperatures fuel several large storms. The first storm, before the 10th, blankets parts of the northeast with a foot of heavy and wet snow, causing travel mayhem for airports from Philadelphia to Boston. Another storm arriving from the west will bring further drought relief to California and then head east. Its impact will be sudden in the Deep South, where an outbreak of tornadoes, common with the onset of El Niño, occurs. The Great Lakes and Northern Plains remain dry and cold early, before turning milder after a brief blizzard from the Dakotas to Minnesota late in the month.

APRIL 2015. A tranquil time of balmy breezes and gentle rains brings the promise of spring to the East. Snow all but disappears, save for the highest northeast peaks where the annual runoff is underway. East winds limit sunshine near the coast for days, with sunshine limited to mid-afternoon. Thunderstorms are strong and prevalent from the Ohio Valley into the Deep South, accompanied by gusty winds and an isolated tornado. Still rainfall is plentiful, promising a fine growing season ahead. A similar picture is found throughout the West Coast, where recent drought conditions ease. Late season snow is heavy in the northern Rockies. Snow also falls in northern Michigan and Wisconsin.

MAY 2015. Hastening the pace to full spring conditions, sunshine is abundant in the East with bright, warm days and cool nights. The threat from frost ends in most places, although its risks linger near the Canadian border. An extended growing season is underway in the far West, courtesy of abundant early spring snow and rain. Any threat from severe weather becomes confined to the Northern Plains, where a few hail-producing thunderstorms can be expected. Misty and cool conditions are slow to lift in coastal New England, while the interior basks in sunshine. Generally, delightful spring weather can be expected for much of the country.

SUMMER

JUNE 2015. Stable early summer weather covers the nation during the month ahead and warmth gently spreads. Gentle breezes infiltrate the harbors of the East and West Coasts, keeping storms muted and temperatures pleasant. An exception occurs on Florida's coastlines where summer thunderstorms begin. Some may be raucous with vivid lightning and torrential rainfall. In the far North along the Canadian border severe weather brings the threat of tornadoes. Great water flows greet early season travelers to the west's national parks where a lingering snow pack is evident along the Continental divide and Sierra Nevada mountain range.

JULY 2015. Summer heat builds to its most robust by the 21st in most places — the exceptions include the Pacific Northeast and New England, where lingering ocean breezes refresh. While the Southeast sizzles, strong Atlantic high pressure brings a southeast wind and numerous downpours from Atlanta northward through the Appalachians. An early season Pacific hurricane also initiates the monsoon season in the Southwest with billowing after clouds yielding brief downpours and gusty winds at higher elevations. Crop yield improves in California and drought relief is evident from robust river flows.

AUGUST 2015. While the air hangs heavy throughout many parts of the country, cool air stirs in the far north by mid-month. Continued low solar activity leads to a cool summer in many places and a slow start to the hurricane season. This can lead to a dusting of snow in the Rockies' highest peaks, a rare sight so early in the season. Thunderstorms are more frequent in the Northeast as several cold fronts pass during an otherwise dry weather pattern. The West Coast enjoys a consistent spell of pleasant weather with the usual variant daily temperatures between closely spaced communities in the Bay Area and southern California, where marine influences are in effect daily. Residents should monitor the fire threat regularly.

AUTUMN

SEPTEMBER 2015. Though the number of Atlantic-born hurricanes is likely to remain subdued, it is still wise to remain vigilant along the East Coast, an area always vulnerable at this time of year. On occasion, long track hurricanes may cause great damage far in excess of that caused by Hurricane Sandy. The natural cyclic nature of land falling major hurricanes capable of producing near catastrophic damage occurs about every 50 years. We are reminded that the great 1938 hurricane uprooted or destroyed about one in every three trees in existence at that time in New England. Given the inevitable recurrence of such a storm,

residents there should remain mindful of its possibility at this time of year.

OCTOBER 2015. October air is crisp and fresh as shadows lengthen and nights become longer. A hint of the season to come is prefaced by a brief snowfall atop New England's highest peaks by mid-month, just as the fall colors arrive. This is generally a dry time across the countryside as the harvest nears completion. Several tropical waves bring brief heavy rainfall to Florida. First frosts are felt across the northern Great Lake states and the Rockies. Unusual and early cold spreads into the Western Plateau region, just as a storm arrives from the Pacific, bringing snow by Halloween to California's Sierra Nevada and briefly subduing the fire danger at lower elevations.

NOVEMBER 2015. An end to the harvest signals a time to prepare for winter, likely to be quite cold again for many. A decade or more of cooling is likely to continue until a meaningful increase in sunspots occurs. Temperatures are likely to remain below east of the Rockies this month with generally dry weather. Several weak disturbances will move quickly across the north with a dusting of snow by mid-month near the Canadian border and the highest peaks in the Rockies. Rainfall will be more widespread in the south, however, including Florida where the fire danger is reduced. California's hillside turns green from welcome rain, progressing from the Bay Area southward during the month.

WINTER

DECEMBER 2015. Icy winds return with the risk of an early frost by mid-month, as far south as northern Florida. A snowfall can be expected from Chicago to the Ohio Valley, blanketing the area with as much as a half-foot. West Coast storms become more frequent as gales sweep Portland and Seattle around the 20th. Farther south, heavy rain causes local flooding along the coastal range. Wet weather ranges as far south as Los Angeles. An extended spell of cool and damp weather can be expected along the Gulf Coast. Yule time will be snow-covered in many parts of the Northeast.

JANUARY 2016. In recent years, deep snow packs have been common in January over a wide area of the United States. This month is likely to bring a different kind of weather pattern to the country. Dry and bitter cold is likely for much of the country with normal temperatures confined to the West Coast. Elsewhere readings are likely to average well below normal, despite a thin snow cover. Great Lake ice coverage will be extensive again, beginning in mid-January. Several ocean storms will graze the East Coast with a blizzard risk over southern New England, including Cape Cod. Lake-effect snow blankets Syracuse and Cleveland, accompanied by howling northwest winds. The Northern Plains remain in the deep freeze much of the time.

FEBRUARY 2016. Snows come late to the East and the nation's heartland this year as the cold somewhat eases. Several powerful storms will bring heavy snow to Chicago and Detroit and a day or so later from Washington to Portland, Maine. The defined storm path this month that will repeat three times originates on the West Coast, bringing wind swept rain there, across the southern Rockies and then to the east. This pattern will likely bring the heaviest inter-mountain snowfall from Colorado to New Mexico. An outbreak of severe weather, including tornadoes, will accompany the second of these storms in the southeast.

THE DIAMOND WAY

The Dorje or Vajra

THE TIBETAN WORD *dorje* (also transliterated as *dorji*) is synonymous with the Sanskrit word *vajra*. No single equivalent English word encapsulates their complex and multi-layered meanings and, so, *vajra* and *dorje* have entered our language. The Sanskrit and Tibetan words are frequently used interchangeably, as they are in this article. Their definitions encompass the literal and the esoteric. The word dorje may be interpreted literally as:

◈ A bolt of lightning or thunder;

◈ A phallus

◈ A diamond.

◈ A specific type of scepter, weapon, and ritual tool.

In addition, transcending these literal meanings, "dorje" and "vajra" may also be interpreted esoterically. Further definitions include:

◈ The state of enlightenment

◈ Adamantine or diamond-hard indestructible wisdom

◈ The eureka moment: that perfect piercing moment of epiphany or diamond-clear clarity

◈ Divine inspiration

◈ Vital essence and fertility: the capacity to generate life

◈ Death

◈ Apocalypse

It's crucial to comprehend that the word "dorje" doesn't merely possess multiple, contradictory meanings. Instead, it simultaneously encompasses *all* of these definitions. This is exemplified by the sacred object that bears its name.

Adamantine scepter

The dorje or vajra is a ritual tool used in Buddhism, Hinduism, and Jainism. It symbolically merges the spiritual powers of a diamond with those of the thunder or lightning bolt, so that indestructibility merges with divine, irresistible force.

In Western culture, diamonds are typically associated with romance, marriage, and expense, as epitomized by the song, "Diamonds are a Girl's Best Friend." The spiritual aspects of the dorje, however, are priceless. In Himalayan cosmology, diamonds are considered flawless, pure, and indestructible — adamantine, in every sense of that word. Just as the diamond is at the top of the Mohs scale, which compares the hardness of minerals by measuring their capacity to scratch others lower on the scale, so the dorje is spiritually and magically able to cut through everything including ignorance and illusion.

History of the vajra

The word "vajra" is first documented in the Rig Veda, although many scholars believe that both concept and tool may have existed earlier. The Rig Veda, a collection of Vedic Sanskrit hymns, is considered among the oldest surviving texts written in an Indo-European language and is roughly dated to between 1700 – 900 BCE. (Scholars disagree about its history, with some claiming the texts to be even older.) In the Rig Veda, the vajra is the sacred attribute and weapon of Indra, Lord of Heaven, the Vedic master of thunderstorms and fertility, spirit of justice and guardian of humanity. Some trace its shape back to the trident.

Indra was the most prominent deity of Vedic India, the equivalent of Zeus or Jupiter in the Greek and Roman pantheons respectively. Like his fellow deities, Indra throws lightning and thunder bolts. Eventually his role diminished in direct proportion to the rise in popularity of the Trimurtri (Brahma, Vishnu, and Shiva). Indra's vajra was used to bless and fertilize Earth, but also to smite enemies and demons. According to a Buddhist legend, Shakyamuni, the historical Buddha, took Indra's vajra and forced its open prongs to close, thus creating a peaceful, spiritual weapon.

Components

The vajra described in the Rig Veda is a thousand-pronged metal club. The modern vajra remains as spiritually potent, but possesses a more modest appearance. The dorje is made in varying sizes and is typically crafted from brass or bronze. It consists of several components. At its center is a sphere, surrounding a shaft that is pointed at each terminus. Emerging from either end of the vajra are spokes that form the shape of lotus flowers. The number of spokes typically ranges from one to nine. They emanate like flames from

Indra, the god of the firmament or atmosphere. The upper half of his body is covered with eyes. He is mounted on his elephant Airâvata.

the mouth of a *makara*, a mythical sea creature, closely associated with the Ganges River and known in Tibetan as a *chu-srin*.

Most dorjes are two-sided, but a double-dorje — two dorjes that are connected to form a cross shape —is known as a *vishva-vajra*. The vishva-vajra has four heads and may be interpreted as representing the Buddhas of the four directions. It may also be interpreted as representing the four rites or activities of Tantra: pacifying, enriching, subjugating, and destroying.

Vajrayana and Shunyata

Vajrayana may be translated literally and variously as Diamond Vehicle, Diamond Road, Lightning Road, or Thunderbolt Way. It refers to Tantric or Esoteric Buddhism. The name, Vajrayana, derives from "vajra" and that object is the quintessential symbol of this spiritual tradition.

The vajra also represents Shunyata, a Buddhist concept that may be translated as the void, emptiness, or openness. Shunyata refers to the primordial nature of the world and the underlying unity of everything. In addition, in Tibetan ritual, the dorje, represents the male principle and is frequently paired with a bell (*dril bu* in Tibetan), which symbolizes the female. Not surprisingly, perhaps, Dorje is a popular men's name in Tibet.

Sacred beings

The dorje is identified with many sacred beings, particularly those of Tibetan Buddhism. It serves as an attribute — an object so closely identified with a sacred being as to serve as identification. "Vajra" or "dorje" is also incorporated into the names of various sacred beings, male and female, including dakinis, Buddhas, and bodhisattvas:

Vajra Nairatmya (Dorje Dagmema): the Lady of Emptiness or the Egoless One is a Buddha and primary Tantric deity.

Phyagna Dorje (Vajrapani): the Diamond Thunderbolt Bearer, among the three principal defenders of the Buddha, may also be an avatar of Indra or even Indra in disguise.

Dorje Pakmo (Vajrayogini): the Diamond Sow is among the most significant *yidam* or sacred meditation beings.

Dorje Rolangma (Vajra Vetali): depending on perspective, the Diamond Zombie or Adamantine Ghoul is a Buddha, dakini, and extremely significant Tantric deity. She vanquishes fear, especially of death and dying.

Vajrabhairava (Yamantaka, Shinjeshe): epitomizing the victory of knowledge and wisdom over death, the Diamond Terror may be a wrathful form of the bodhisattva Manjushri. He may be Shiva in disguise or he may be an indigenous Tibetan spirit converted to the dharma.

– JUDIKA ILLES

The Birds of Somerset

THE OLD FOLKS tell that crows are harbingers of evil, for, if one is seen flying alone, it betokens ill-luck and to see one perched in the path is a sign of wrath and dismay. Offer the crow respect when you see one, but at all costs, avoid crossing its path.

The screech of an owl is still heard with alarm: "the owl's screech is a sound of death to the body."

Cuckoos come in for their share of patronage, for when the cry of one is heard for the first time, it is usual to turn the money in the pocket and with children often sing:

Cuckoo, cuckoo, cherry tree,
Catch a penny and give it to me.

The robin is held in great veneration. To kill one is deemed unlucky. Before the death of a person, this bird is said to be seen tapping three times at the window.

The wren was sacred in the eyes of the Druids and therefore is also treated with great respect. The praises of both wren and robin are sung in the old couplet:

The robin and the wren
are God Almighty's cock and hen.

Fireflies

ON A HOT summer night, just as dusk descends, at the edge of a wood or marsh, something magical happens. As the sunlight fades, small twinkles of light, faint at first, pulse in the growing shadows. As night overtakes the twilight, more flashes appear, glowing brighter against the contrast of the deepening dark.

Imagine seeing this spectacle for the first time. What would you think you were seeing? Early man often attributed supernatural causes to lights that appear in the dark. Some thought that the slim flying beetles with bioluminescent abdomens responsible for the rhythmic flashes you see were faeries.

Legends

A Filipino legend held that the light emanated from torches that the tiny creatures carried to scare away fruit bats, who would otherwise eat them. Yet another legend from the same country states that a humble fly found a king's lost ring and as a reward asked to have a light, so that he might visit his friends at night. The wish was granted. In one part of Mexico, people believed that the lights were from witches or wizards who threw fire as they flew through the night.

The humble firefly has a role in the creation myth of the Mewan people, who lived in what we now know as California. As people began to multiply and populate the land, they had an increasing need of fire for food and warmth. Two brother shrews were sent on a mission to steal some fire from Crow. Catching a spark that flew out from the smoke hole of Crow's house, they stowed it in a buckskin bag. Before running off with their treasure, they pushed a bug backward into the buckskin until the poor bug touched the spark. The magic spark did not harm the bug, but instead endowed it with a light which guided them back to the waiting tribe.

Firefly Omens

An old Italian superstition held that the *lucciole* (fireflies) were the souls of the departed. If a firefly entered the home, some would mourn them, as one would mourn the dead, thinking they must surely be a relative come back from the grave. Others would react in fear, thinking them messengers of the grave, come to announce an impending death.

94

Not all firefly visitations foretell bad fortune. Some people believe that a firefly in the home means you will have an unexpected visitor the following day. A variation on this belief is that there will be one person more, or one fewer, the next day. That is, someone will come, or someone will go.

If there is a single person living in the house, two fireflies indicate an upcoming marriage. If there are no single people, two fireflies mean good luck for all who dwell within. Several fireflies in the house indicate even more good luck in the form of a party in the near future.

Encouraging Fireflies

Fireflies, even without their magical associations, are beautiful — and beneficial. Firefly larvae eat snails, slugs, aphids, and mites.

Provide a welcoming habitat for our mystical friends. Avoid pesticides. If possible, leave some area of your property wild; allow the grass to grow a little longer. Plant trees. Allow forest litter to accumulate. Take care, though, for some of the methods for attracting fireflies also encourages mosquitoes and ticks. Your local wildlife or agricultural authority might be able to help you decide what's appropriate in your area.

There is one thing you can do, though, to encourage fireflies without encouraging pests: Turn off outside lights at night. Firefly flashes are part of an intricate mating signal. Lights from houses and passing cars can interfere with breeding.

And when the outside lights are off, and the moon is hidden, wait and watch. And imagine, if you will, that they are indeed fairies, and enjoy the display.

– Morven Westfield

95

Mystical Number Sequences

111, 222, 333, 444, 555, 666, 777, 888, 999

THEY APPEAR when least expected and inspire wonder. When repeating number sequences are observed, they frequently give pause. Typically the numbers come in threes, a number long-linked to attention and breakthroughs. As the old saying goes, "The third time is the charm."

Following a purchase, the cashier at the grocery store might offer $7.77 in change. The digits 111 or perhaps 333 might appear repeatedly on the clock, addresses, or maybe on the license plates of cars in traffic. Is there a deeper force at work, trying to call attention to something?

Numbers have long imprinted metaphysical practices and spell casting. As well as being omens, these single-number sequences can be employed to enhance the success of magical workings. Here is a guide to the messages encoded in number multiples.

111 — A new door opens. Thoughts manifest. It is time to begin.

Astrologically, one is the number of the sun and Leo. This sequence refers to individuality and finding your identity and will power. It encourages leadership. Adopt a 'take charge' attitude. The triple one accents new beginnings and shows you how to shine.

222 — All will be well in the end. Keep your faith in the powers of good to overcome evil.

Two is the number of the moon and Cancer. It refers to emotional experiences and the need for balance and harmony amid the waxing and waning of fate. Two is the number of partnership.

333 — Higher beings such as saints, angels, and ascended ones offer guidance and protection. This is an omen of growth and good fortune.

Often called the perfect number, three relates to benevolent Jupiter, the planet of expansion and luck. Astrologically, it links with Sagittarius. The three-sequence is a positive message for travel, as well as for animal companions.

444 — Grounding and support are present. The base is solid. Fear not, for help is on the way. Peaceful connections are indicated.

Four — the number of the sides of a square — is about parameters and practicalities. It reminds us to respect tradition and the work ethic in order to assure a predictable outcome. Saturn and Capricorn are the astrological affiliations.

555 — Growth and creativity abound. There is a sense of rebirth and released potentials. Expect transformation and a series of changes too.

Five is mercurial. Ideas, duality, and restlessness will prevail when it appears as a multiple. Mercury, Gemini, and Virgo are the astrological ties.

666 — There is a need for balance. Don't let material and selfish motives rule you. Be true and idealistic.

As the Mark of the Beast, 666 is the traditional biblical number of evil. Selfishness, materialism, sensuality, and indulgence are six at its worst. Think of Miss Piggy. Hopefully that analogy brought a smile to your lips, for humor is the most effective weapon against evil. The message of sequential-six is to face and overcome the negative and possessive side of Venus, so as to find beauty and love. Venus, Taurus, and Libra are the astrological ties.

777 — Rewards arrive, following your good work. Uplift others and you, too, will rise. Celestial and blessed situations arise.

Seven, a prime number, is rich with mystical significance. Think of the seven days of the week, the seven chakras of the body, the rainbow's seven colors, and the seven musical notes of the scale. Biblically, seven is the number of God and the heavens. Divine intervention and unique blessings are manifesting. Uranus and Aquarius are the astrological links to seven.

888 — Generosity and abundance surround you. Timing is good; expect financial success.

Eight is an elegant and powerful number. It marks an entry into places and circumstances of privilege. Business enterprises go well, bringing the freedom to rise above material needs. Reflect upon the cosmic lemniscate, that sideways figure eight which appears in the Tarot and other occult doctrines. Astrologically, Neptune (the higher octave of Venus) and Pisces are affiliated with the eighth vibration.

999 — Do all the good you can: your role is to enlighten others and share your wealth of knowledge. It's a philosophical time.

The nine is a number of elevated consciousness and charity. A cycle of life is culminating, when nines appear. It's an alpha and omega message. Reflect upon how far you have come and what you can share with those who are struggling. The nine asks, "What new heights can you aspire to?" Mars, Aries, Pluto, and Scorpio are the astrological correlations.

Be aware of number sequences and synchronicities when they appear. They offer important messages, reassurance, and encouragement sent by angels and other divine beings.

– DIKKI-JO MULLEN

The Christmas Tree Séance

SOME say that the gloom time is best for contacting the spirit world. The gloom time begins just after the autumn equinox, when darkness begins to fall earlier and earlier each evening. It intensifies at All Hallows when the veil to the other side is thinnest. Ghostly activity is celebrated with pumpkins, costumes and candles. The witcheries of the winter solstice and New Year's Eve include connections with and messages from other dimensions.

Darker, longer evenings often have an atmosphere conducive to psychic awareness. Charles Dickens' classic tale, *A Christmas Carol*, featuring Scrooge and a trio of memorable Christmas spirits, is perhaps the best known and beloved of the many ghost stories associated with the gloom time.

Spiritualists and mediums

A fragrant Christmas tree, lit and decorated, provides a glorious and powerful focus for evoking memories of holidays past, as well as anticipated joys to come. During the late nineteenth century, Spiritualists — those dedicated to offering messages of survival and hope from the afterlife — began to hold séance sessions featuring Christmas trees. This practice is still popular today. England's famous Arthur Findlay School, which offers a variety of metaphysical programs, including training and certification for mediums, promotes a Christmas tree séance during the winter holidays.

Mediums — those highly sensitive individuals who have developed an ability to connect with the spirit world — use the energy and ambiance of the Christmas tree as a focus during these special events. The result is a particularly enjoyable and impressive type of séance. A great deal of paranormal phenomena tends to take place. Laughter, voices, apparitions, and telekinetic activity have been noticed by those in attendance.

Preparing the séance

After preparing the Christmas tree, perhaps including vintage ornaments along with traditional sparkling, festive decorations, a variety of unwrapped toys for both boys and girls of all ages should be heaped around the tree's base.

Music and singing are incorporated into these séances to heighten the energy and welcome spirit visitors. The musical selections should be traditional holiday songs. The participants will sit in a semi-circle, so that everyone can see both the medium who is conducting the séance and the beautiful tree.

Christmas tree séances tend to attract the spirits of children who have died, which can be of particular comfort to grieving parents who have lost a little one. However, adults who especially loved Christmas have also appeared.

A Floridian séance

A few years back, at a private Christmas tree séance held by a Floridian witch, the voices of at least fifty children were heard, laughing and shouting in delight as they drifted in from the spirit world to inspect the tree and choose their toys. A toy trumpet kept blasting at intervals, an argument over who was to have a large doll, and another voice asking for a bicycle were heard. Favorite siblings and other relatives are often called by affectionate and familiar nicknames by the spectral visitors.

Christmas tree séances tend to be lengthy. After about two hours, the toys will usually be left scattered all around the room in innocent and loving disarray. The spirit children will take astral forms and impressions of the toys with them. The physical toys left behind seem to be blessed with a benevolent and gentle energy. It's good to donate them to needy children for Christmas gifts.

– ESTHER ELAYNE

Magical Hedgerows

FOR THE ancient Celts, all boundaries were liminal, magical places; whether the boundary between day and night (dawn, dusk), between the water and the land, or the portals between summer and winter (Beltaine and Samhain). The same applied to boundaries in the landscape. Offerings such as bog butter were often left for the Spirits of Place, at the spot where two landholdings met.

In Scottish tradition, it was important to *saine* (sanctify or purify) the boundaries of your land yearly, by "walking the bounds" with a flaming torch, making a sun-wise circuit. The house, the barn, the herds, and the land could also be *sained* with salt or salt water, especially water taken from the ninth wave of the sea.

According to the ancient Irish Brehon Laws, a boundary could be marked by a standing stone, or large natural rock, a ditch, a tree, water, or a roadway. Another sturdy boundary marker was the living hedge or hedgerow.

Hedgerows have been around since the Neolithic farming revolution (4,000 – 6,000 years ago), to protect the crops and animals from predators. Bronze Age and Iron Age peoples also made walls of living plants, often using plants with thorns, as their version of modern barbed wire. Hedgerows might incorporate trees or be made of bushes or vines. Ideally the structure was half-earth and half-hedge. A dirt wall lay at the base, shored up with stones laid against it, to prevent erosion and stop animals like rabbits from burrowing into the sides.

Making a Hedgerow

If a hedgerow is made of trees, they should be planted about thirty feet apart, to permit enough sun for growth, and the distances should be staggered for a more natural effect. If the hedgerow is made of bushes, these can be trimmed regularly to promote bushy growth — but it may take a few years for the hedge to produce fruit and flowers after trimming. Interweaving or pleaching is done by making cuts at the base of stems and bending the branches between wooden stakes to form a woven wall of vegetation.

The mystical aspects of the trees and shrubs used in boundary marking should always be considered, especially if your hedgerow is designed to protect a sacred enclosure. Consider a mix of species, so that your hedge will provide flowers, fruits, and showy foliage throughout the year.

Here are samplings of useful hedge plants that will provide food and medicine for animals and people, as well as protect the sacred boundaries of the land.

Hedge Plants suitable for Southern areas

New Jersey Tea, Red Root
(Ceanothus americanus)
Deer will relish the twigs in winter and the white flowers attract butterflies. The seeds are eaten by wild turkeys and quail. The leaves can be used as a beverage tea, the root and flowers can be used as dyes, and the bark of the root benefits colds, fevers, snake bites, and stomach aches, spleen inflammation, and lung conditions such as asthma and bronchitis. The root bark tea can also help to lower blood pressure. The flowers were used by Native American women as a fragrant body wash in preparation for marriage.

Hibiscus or Rose Mallow
(Hibiscus rosa-sinensis)
A woody shrub with large flowers of different colors, depending upon the species and age of the plant. The flowers attract bees, butterflies, and hummingbirds and are made into a delicious beverage tea that contains vitamin C and minerals, acts as a refrigerant (brings down the temperature in

fevers), and lowers blood pressure. White flowering hibiscus is an herb of the moon. Pink and red flowering hibiscus belong to Venus.

Camellia
(C. japonica, C. reticulata, C. sasanqua and others)
These shrubs provide lovely, fragrant flowers and have the advantage of blooming in late fall, winter and early spring. Camellias are an herb of the moon.

Orange Jessamine, Mock Orange
(Murraya paniculata)
An evergreen, tropical, white flowered tree that, in some species, produces small orange or red fruits. In tropical areas, the tree blooms year round, attracting bees and birds. (A similar plant for more northern areas is the gardenia bush). The leaf extract has been used to treat diarrhea and inflammation. For the Javanese, this herb is a symbol of wisdom and is said to protect the house from bad luck. It is used in wedding ceremonies to bring a joyful union and in funerals to make a fragrant bed for the deceased.

North American Hedge Plants

Trifoliate Orange, Chinese Bitter Orange
(Poncirus trifoliata)
This citrusy plant is hardy to Zone 5 and tolerates frost and snow. It is thorny, deciduous (drops its leaves in winter), bears fragrant leaves and flowers, and has small orange bitter fruits that can be used for marmalade. "Flying Dragon" is a variety with interesting, twisted stems.

The fruits are used to relieve allergic inflammation in Chinese medicine and show anti-tumor and anti-viral properties. They contain Vitamin C and can be juiced to help with colds. Oranges symbolize the sun, luck, and good fortune and are said to attract good business. The flowers are used in weddings to bring good fortune and happiness and added to the bath to make one more alluring. Oranges may be used to invoke Apollo, Hera, and Gaia.

Apothecary's Rose
(Rosa gallica var. officinalis)
The advantage of this variety is that it can tolerate semi-shade. Rose hips are soothing to mucus linings in the throat and intestinal tract, and contain Vitamin C to boost the immune system and ward off colds. The flowers are very fragrant and the scent of rose is a natural anti-depressant. The petals can be used as a beverage tea, in jellies, as a douche, and to wash sore eyes. Rose is an herb of the moon and belongs to Venus. Roses symbolize love, beauty, and joy, and bring passion to a wedding or hand-fasting.

Barberry
(Berberis vulgaris)
This thorny bush produces yellow flowers in the spring and showy berries in the fall that turn from green to yellow to red. The berries are edible and rich in Vitamin C. They contain a good amount of pectin and are used to help jams jell. They are added to rice pilaf in Iran. The ripe berries are used in teas and syrups to treat colds, flu, fever, and infections and may be rubbed on sore gums. The fall-gathered bark of the root is a liver medicine. The berries, root, or leaves can be sewn into an amulet for protection from evil. Barberry is an herb of Mars.

Hawthorn *(Crataegus spp.)*
This tree was an important one for the Druids, who would watch for the blooming of the hawthorn to announce the festival of Beltaine (May Day).The timing was important because once the  hawthorns in their area had bloomed, they knew it was warm enough to send the cattle between the Beltaine ritual fires and up into the hills. The young leaves and flowers are tinctured in alcohol in the spring and the red fruits are tinctured in the fall to make a cardiac tonic that helps regulate blood pressure, myocarditis, atherosclerosis, stress, insomnia, and nervous tension. Tradition tells us that where oak and ash and thorn are found together one is most likely to see Fairies. Hawthorn is an herb of Mars.

Blackberry
(Rubus villosus)
Walking along country roads in Ireland, you may come upon large hedges of blackberry. The thorny bush provides protection for the farm and luscious fruits for jams, jellies, and ice cream. The berries are slightly astringent and help with diarrhea; the bark of the root is a much stronger ant-diarrheal. The leaves are applied to burns to relieve pain and chewed to help

bleeding gums. Blackberries are sacred to Brighid, a triple fire goddess. This is an old healing charm used when applying the leaves to a burn;

Three ladies come from the east,
One with fire and two with frost.
Out with fire and in with frost.
Blackberry is an herb of Venus.

Shadbush, Serviceberry, Juneberry, Amelanchier
(Amelanchier spp.)
Juneberry species have differing qualities; some are bushes and some are small trees. They produce white, pink, yellow, or red streaked flowers in early spring, at the time of the shad run. The flowering of these trees was once a signal to Native American tribes in New England that it was time to go fishing. In Appalachia, their blooming meant that roads were again passable and that the ground was thawed enough

to bury those who had died over the winter. In the plains, the blue berries heralded the return of the blue birds from their winter nesting grounds.

As the name implies, the bushes produce blueberry-like fruits in June that can be eaten raw or made into pie or jam. They can also be added to breads, muffins, salads, granola, and pancakes. They can be frozen on a cookie sheet and then kept frozen in a container for later use.

Juneberry Sauce *(for pancakes, cheese cake, ice cream, etc.)*
1 cup Juneberries
½ cup water
½ cup sugar

1 tbsp. lemon juice
2 tbsp. corn starch
Place in a small saucepan and stir continuously while heating, until a thick sauce results.

Native Americans used the berries to make pemmican, a mixture of fruits, chopped dry meat, and fat. Moths and butterflies appreciate the leaves and deer and rabbits will browse the branches. The wood was once used to make arrow shafts, tool handles and fishing rods.

Sea-Buckthorn, Hippophae
(Hippophae rhamnoides)
Another plant that makes a great barrier hedge or windbreak with colorful, edible berries and strong roots that will hold back soil. Common along sandy sea coasts in Europe, the plant also thrives in desert areas of Asia. It needs full sun to thrive and be sure you have both male and female plants; the female plant produces the orange berries that are an important winter food for birds and also useful for us humans.

The branches have thorns, which makes harvesting a challenge. An old technique was to break off an entire branch, freeze it, and then shake off the berries. The berries were then kept frozen for later use. A less destructive method is to shake the branches to allow the berries to drop onto a cloth.

The berries are bitter and taste best after they have been frozen. The juice of the vitamin C and A-rich fresh berries can be added to other sweeter juices, such as apple, to improve flavor. The fruits can also be used to make jams, pies and fruit liqueurs, mead and wine. The fruits benefit the lungs, digestive tract, heart, liver, skin, reproductive organs, and metabolism and are anti-inflammatory. The leaves and bark are astringent and used to treat wounds, suppuration, and bleeding externally, and diarrhea internally. Sea-Buckthorn is an herb of Saturn that is said to foster communication with animals, especially between a horse and rider.

Caution: the leaves and bark are not for long term use internally, due to their high tannin content.

Mountain Ash, Rowan
(Sorbus americana, S. aucuparia)
This is the ultimate tree for magical protection, according to Scottish lore, with lovely white flowers in the spring and bright red or orange berries in the fall. Rowan branches were once placed in the cradle, hung over the door, and over the entrance to the barn to protect against sorcery. Planted near the home, Rowan is said to be protective against fire. Planted near graveyards, it keeps the dead from rising. Walk with a rowan stick to safely enter Fairy forts and to avoid being "taken" by the Fairies. Highland ladies once wore necklaces of red rowan berries as a form of magical protection. Rowan is an herb of the moon.

The berries are rich in Vitamin C and were once made into syrup with apples and honey, for fevers, bronchitis, and other lung ailments. The berries should be picked after the first frost, when they have a deep, bright color. A teaspoon of the fresh juice in water can be used as a gargle for mouth sores and sore throats. (If dried berries are used, first soak them in water for ten hours to soften). The berries are made into jam that will help treat diarrhea in adults and children. The jam is also used as a condiment for meats, such as wild game and lamb.

Rowan Berry Jam
Place equal parts ripe rowan berries and finely chopped apples, including the cores, into a pan. Bring to a simmer and cook until the fruit is soft (the berries will lose their color).

When the fruit is soft enough, press through a sieve and then discard the seeds and skins.

Place one part organic sugar (or one-half part honey) into a separate pan with a little water and simmer until the sugar dissolves.

Bring the sugar water to a boil, add the pulp, and bring back to a boil. Boil for five more minutes. Test by dropping the jam onto a plate and see if, when cooled, it forms sticky ridges.

Caution: children should not eat the raw berries but they may safely eat the jam.

English Holly
(Ilex aquifolium)
This hedge plant makes a dense evergreen wall with lovely white flowers and later, the classic red berries. It has leaves that can be used as tea for coughs, colds, flu, and bronchitis. Holly tea

also benefits gout, bladder conditions, and arthritic complaints. Simmer two tablespoons of leaf per cup of water for 20 minutes in a non-aluminum pot with a tight lid. A 150 pound adult may take ¼ cup four times a day (adjust the dosage according to body weight).

Caution: make sure you are using English holly and not another holly species because some species are emetic (they will cause vomiting). The berries are poisonous.

Prickly holly is a warrior herb. Make holly water by steeping the herb in water under the full moon and sprinkle the water on any person, place, or thing in need of protection; use it to bless a newborn, etc. Holly is placed on the door at Winter Solstice, as a symbol that the nature spirits are welcome into your home. Holly is an herb of Mars.

Lavender
(Lavandula vera, L. officinalis)
Single hardy flower species such as lavender have been used to mark boundaries in some areas. Plant a thick row of winter hardy lavender on a raised earthen bank, shored up with flat stones along the base. Lavender tea is a natural anti-depressive and the scent is calming to those in pain. Bring lavender into your home to foster peace, love, and healing. The flowers have antiseptic qualities and can be added to herbal salves. The leaf tea helps with nausea and vomiting.

Steep two teaspoons of the flowers per cup of water for 20 minutes; a 150 pound adult may take ¼ cup four times a day (adjust the dosage depending upon the weight of the person)

Lavender flowers and rose petals can be soaked in vinegar for a few weeks and then strained. The vinegar is applied to the temples and forehead, using a compress, to soothe headaches. An ingredient of love spells, the scent of lavender is said to attract men. Offer the flowers to the Midsummer fire, to honor the Gods and Goddesses. Lavender is an herb of Mercury, especially sacred to Hecate and Saturn.

– ELLEN HOPMAN

Planetary Hours

♄ ♃ ♂ ☉ ♀ ☿ ☽

TIMING PLAYS a crucial factor in the success of magical workings. Most old grimoires focus closely on the timing of rites. Many such as *The Goetia* and *The Heptameron* utilize the system of planetary hours, which have been in persistent use since at least the Middle Ages. These are not "hours" in the modern sense.

Planetary hours reference the traditional seven planets visible to the naked eye. As the system was devised before there were adequate telescopes, Uranus, Neptune, and Pluto are not included, but the sun and moon are, although modern science no longer considers these luminaries to be planets.

The list of planetary hours is as follows: Saturn, Jupiter, Mars, Sun, Venus, Mercury, Moon.

The ordering of this list of planets is not random, nor accidental. Instead, the order is derived from the perceived movement of these heavenly bodies from Earth, from slowest to fastest — in other words, from Saturn, the slowest, to the moon, the quickest. Those familiar with Qabalah will note that the Tree of Life's Sephirot follow the exact same pattern, beginning with Binah (corresponding to Saturn) down to Yesod (the moon).

Each day of the week was perceived as ruled by a planet:
Sunday: the sun
Monday: the moon
Tuesday: Mars
Wednesday: Mercury
Thursday: Jupiter
Friday: Venus
Saturday: Saturn

Occultists further divided days and nights into twelve sections, respectively. The day hours start at sunrise, with the first hour ruled by that day's planetary ruler. Subsequent rulers follow this pattern of movement. Night hours begin at sunset, but follow the pattern established at dawn. For example, the first hour on a Tuesday starts at sunrise and is ruled by Mars. The next hour is ruled by the sun; the following by Venus, and so forth. The hour of

Saturn follows that of the moon.

Here's the pattern for a typical Tuesday:

First hour (day): Mars
Second hour (day): Sun
Third hour (day): Venus
Fourth hour (day): Mercury
Fifth hour (day): Moon
Sixth hour (day): Saturn
Seventh hour (day): Jupiter
Eighth hour (day): Mars
Ninth hour (day): Sun
Tenth hour (day): Venus
Eleventh hour (day): Mercury
Twelfth hour (day): Moon
First hour (night): Saturn
Second hour (night): Jupiter
Third hour (night): Mars
Fourth hour (night): Sun
Fifth hour (night): Venus
Sixth hour (night): Mercury
Seventh hour (night): Moon
Eighth hour (night): Saturn
Ninth hour (night): Jupiter
Tenth hour (night): Mars
Eleventh hour (night): Sun
Twelfth hour (night): Venus

The following planet is Mercury, the ruler of the first hour (the dawn) of Wednesday. This is actually a pretty simple way to check your calculations: if you go through the entire pattern, but find yourself with an incompatible dawn hour (say Venus at dawn on a Saturday), then you know that you have messed up somewhere along the way and must recalculate.

Dividing the hours is really the only tricky part and involves some basic math. Grab a calculator for the next step. You also need to know the time of sunrise and sunset on the date in question.

Example

This was written in Providence, Rhode Island, on Thursday, the sixth day of October, 2011. At this location and on this day, the sun rose at 6:48 AM and set at 6:19 PM. Plenty of online databases catalog local sunrise and sunset times. You can also check a local newspaper.

As the sun rises at 6:48 AM and sets at 6:19 PM, we have approximately eleven hours and thirty-one minutes of daylight to work with. Calculated in minutes alone, there are six-hundred ninety-one minutes altogether (11×60=660. 660+31=691). Divide this number (691) by 12, which yield 57.58. Therefore, each "day hour" will be approximately 57.58 minutes long.

The night hours are calculated in similar manner. Since there are 1440 minutes in a full 24 hour period (24×60=1440), merely subtract the number of day minutes (691) from 1440 to yield 749. Then divide 749 by 12 to get 62.42 minutes. Therefore, each night hour is approximately 62.42 minutes long. A way to check your math is to add the day hour length to the night hour length. If the numbers do not add up to 120, something is amiss in your calculations.

From this point, it is merely a matter of addition. The first day hour begins at sunrise (in this case, 6:48 AM), and will end 57.58 minutes later. To add this easily, we add 48 and 57.58 together, yielding 105.58, and then subtract 60, which is 45.58. So our second day hour begins at approximately 7:46 AM.

For the next hour, we follow the same process. 45.58 + 57.58 = 103.16. Subtract 60 and we have 43.16. Our next day hour thus begins at 8:43 AM. This process is then repeated until sunset. It is important to keep using the decimal integers in your calculations to keep them accurate (i.e. 43.16 as opposed to merely 43) since numbers can vary considerably, after only a few calculations. If done correctly, your list should look like the one below. Since these calculations are for Thursday, our first hour is ruled by Jupiter.

1st Day Hour 6:48 – 7:46: Jupiter
2nd Day Hour 7:46 – 8:43: Mars
3rd Day Hour 8:43 – 9:41: Sun
4th Day Hour 9:41 – 10:38: Venus
5th Day Hour 10:38 – 11:36: Mercury
6th Day Hour 11:36 – 12:33: Moon
7th Day Hour 12:33 – 1:31: Saturn
8th Day Hour 1:31 – 2:29: Jupiter
9th Day Hour 2:29 – 3:26: Mars
10th Day Hour 3:26 – 4:24: Sun
11th Day Hour 4:24 – 5:21: Venus
12th Day Hour 5:21 – 6:19: Mercury

Note that the last minute of our 12th hour coincides perfectly with the time of sunset. This is another way to check your work. If your final day hour does not end at sunset, there is a mistake and you must recalculate.

The night hours

The night hours follow the same pattern, except that 62.42 is our target number of minutes. Starting with 19 (or, more specifically, 18.96), add 62.42 and get 81.38, then subtract the 60 and get 21.38. So, our second night hour begins at 7:21 PM. Continue the process and we get:

1st Night Hour 6:19 – 7:21: Moon
2nd Night Hour 7:21 – 8:24: Saturn
3rd Night Hour 8:24 – 9:26: Jupiter
4th Night Hour 9:26 – 10:29: Mars
5th Night Hour 10:29 – 11:31: Sun
6th Night Hour 11:31 – 12:33: Venus
7th Night Hour 12:33 – 1:36: Mercury
8th Night Hour 1:36 – 2:38: Moon
9th Night Hour 2:38 – 3:41: Saturn
10th Night Hour 3:41 – 4:43: Jupiter
11th Night Hour 4:43 – 5:46: Mars
12th Night Hour 5:46 – 6:48: Sun

We now have both day and night planetary hours, beginning at dawn on October 6th, 2011 for Providence, RI.

Note how our 12th night hour ended precisely at 6:48 AM, that is, the time of sunrise. This is yet another way to check whether calculations are accurate.

However, keep in mind that sunrise the next day may be a minute or two earlier or later, depending upon time of year. Note also that the next planetary ruler after our twelfth night hour is Venus, the correct ruler for a Friday dawn. This indicates that our table is perfect.

So now what?

To the old school occultists, each planet represented a series of correspondences. For example, Mars rules things concerning war, exercise, strength, power, and martial endeavors. Mercury rules languages, learning, intelligence, and thievery. Venus rules creature comforts, parties, sexual liaisons and the like.

Say a typical renaissance occultist wished to cast a spell in order to procure a new lover. He would probably wait until Friday, the day of Venus, to cast his spell, and would perform it during one of the hours of Venus. He might also consecrate a sigil or magic square of Venus; burn incenses considered sacred to Venus; and possibly even wear something green to help "seal the deal." If, on the other hand, he was interesting in learning a new language as quickly as possible, he would most likely do these things on a Wednesday, during an hour of Mercury, and would work with colors, incense, and sigils associated with that planet instead.

– DIKKI-JO MULLEN

The Planetary Hours   Augsburg (1490)

Wassail

*This recipe features apples, but Wassail may also be made
from berries, pears, or other available fruits:*

Ingredients

1/2 gallon unsweetened apple juice
1/2 gallon hard apple cider
1/2 cup unrefined sugar
1/2 tsp. ground cloves
1 tbsp. powdered ginger
1 tsp. grated nutmeg
1 tsp. ground mace
1 tsp. ground allspice
1 tbsp. ground cinnamon
1 orange
1 tsp. lemon juice
4 apples — cored and peeled
6 cinnamon sticks for stirring
  individual mugs
Brandy or dark ale

Heat the apple juice and cider to just below the boiling point.

Add sugar and stir until it is completely dissolved and then reduce heat to a simmer

Add cloves, ginger, nutmeg, mace, allspice, and cinnamon, and stir until blended.

Add lemon juice and the juice of one orange.

Add the apples one half hour prior to serving. They will float and absorb the flavors of the brew.

Guests can add brandy or dark ale, if desired. Use cinnamon sticks for stirring.

Yule Celebration   Harper's New Monthly Magazine (1871)

The Amazing Oracle Ouija Speaks

The myths and mysteries of Talking Boards

MESSAGES from the afterlife: since earliest times, methods to assure clear communication with the spirit realm have been sought by the living. The quest is both tantalizing and irresistible. Of the variety of oracles employed to seek messages of peace and love from departed loved ones or from angels and other supernatural beings, the Ouija (pronounce it either wee-gee or we-ja) or talking board is perhaps the most controversial. Maybe that is because it can be consulted by anyone at any time. No special training or talent is required, which might be why some professional psychics discourage its use.

Some critics claim that Ouija and its companion boards are the most sinister of games. It has even been said that they are evil gateways, inviting lies and the entry of demonic forces. Staunch proponents and defenders affirm that this is nonsense and that the oracle brings comforting messages and accurate information through contact with loving spirits and divine entities.

Boards and pointers

The Ouija or talking board is a message board with a movable pointer. The board is decorated with letters of the alphabet and the numbers from 0 through 9. The words "Yes" and "No"; "Hello" and "Good Bye"; as well as some mystical illustrations might also be included.

The board is balanced on the laps of two people (a lady and a gentleman preferably), who face each other with knees touching, while they ask questions or make requests. Soon the pointer will begin to move, spelling out a message. Sometimes a single inquirer can work the board, too.

The little plank

Pointers range from an inverted wine glass to a variety of contraptions called planchettes. *Planchette* is a French word meaning "little plank" or "little board." It is often a small, heart-shaped, footed table. More elaborate carved creations with tiny wheels have been used, too.

The questioners will rest all ten fingertips gently on the planchette, then voice questions or concerns, and wait for the device to move. It usually does, often bringing amazing messages, which prove to be true. Critics say this is merely unconscious movements made by those touching the board and planchette, making it merely a vehicle for the power of suggestion. But then, how is it possible to explain why so much information is given that none of the sitters could possibly have known?

THE BOSTON
PLANCHETTE
From the Original Pattern, first made in Boston in 1860.

Revelations from the unseen world

Mystique is part of Ouija's appeal. No one knows quite where talking boards originated or even the source of the name. In metaphysical references, there are many mentions of Ouija's ancient past.

This claim comes from *The Encyclopedia of Psychic Science*: "As an invention it is very old. It was in use in the days of Pythagoras, about 540 BCE According to a French historical account of the philosopher's life, his sect held frequent séances or circles at which a mystic table moving on wheels, moved toward signs, which the philosopher and his pupil, Philolaus interpreted to the audience as being revelations supposedly from the unseen world."

Origins of Ouija

Other authors attribute Ouija's origins to China, Egypt, Greece, Rome, 13th century Tatars and Mongols, as well as other important and interesting cultures. There is even a claim that a well-known French medium, a Madame Planchette (she has never been found), invented the talking board. None of this exotic background has ever been substantiated. No early boards have been unearthed in archeological sites or are mentioned in early texts. Automatic writing, which was practiced in China, is the closest link the ancient world might have to the talking board phenomenon.

Ouija is a true clever and dualistic Gemini: 'born' on May 28, 1890, the day that two businessmen, Elijah Bond and Charles Kennard applied for its patent. Kennard claimed the name Ouija was an ancient Egyptian word meaning good luck. The board grew out of parlor games that appealed to many when Spiritualism developed during the 19th century. Kennard spent his life trying

to prove that he invented Ouija, but in 1901, his employee, William Fuld of Baltimore, Maryland, took over production. Fuld claimed the name was a combination of the French (oui) and German (ja), both words for "yes." Fuld reinvented the history of Ouija and claimed credit for its creation himself. Competitors flooded the market with products named Swami, Angel, Genie, Spook, and similar.

All the answers

The popularity of Ouija, by any other name, skyrocketed during the early years of the 20th century with the continuing widespread belief in Spiritualism. The yearning to connect with deceased or missing loved ones intensified during World War I. Fuld's sales-skill fueled Ouija's success. He told of how the board "knows all of the answers" and that it gave him all of his best ideas.

In 1927, Fuld died suddenly. Some said it was an accidental fall. Others said it was murder — he was engaged in several bitter lawsuits with competitors — or suicide. His mysterious end enhanced Ouija's allure. The game became even more popular, earning

millions of dollars for his heirs, until they sold the patent to Parker Brothers in 1966. Talking boards certainly seem to bring more good luck than bad. They continue to be best sellers, appearing in a variety of guises, today.

Tips and technique

As a longtime fan and enthusiastic supporter of Ouija, here is a technique I've found to help generate the brightest and best experience:

1 Light a white candle.
2. Affirm a tranquil, positive atmosphere.
3. Speak aloud asking that only the highest and the best be allowed to enter.
4. Solemnly and slowly ask a single question at a time.
5. Wait for the pointer to spell an answer. (It can be helpful to have an assistant take note of the letters and numbers indicated.)

– MOTHER OLLMANN

KILL DEVIL

Spirits for the Gods

THE USE of alcoholic beverages to appease the gods and foster communications with them has a long history that spans the globe. To this day, prayers are often accompanied by pouring libations and sharing spirits to gain the favor of deities and ancestral entities. Rum holds a special place among the many beverages offered to beings of the Otherworld. Historically, rum has served as a means of remuneration, a channel for the spirits, and as an offering to attract the favor of various gods across a broad spectrum of societies, territories, and continents

Wherever you find sugar production from cane, rum will also be found. This lusty drink is fermented either directly from cane juice or from molasses, a byproduct of sugar production. The oldest-known "rum" may have originated in Malaysia, approximately one-thousand years ago, in the form of a drink called *brum*. However it would be at least another six centuries before rum would achieve the prominent position that it occupies today.

Spiritual and monetary currency

With the European conquests in the Americas, the enslavement of Africans, and a world economy that depended on sugar as a mainstay, rum became not only a currency of speaking with the gods, but also a literal, monetary currency. However, despite its lucrative trade status, rum's older uses persisted.

Rum, which was at times called "kill devil" in Barbados, was described by one resident a as "hot, hellish, and terrible liquor" that had many diverse uses in various locations. In Western Africa, a child was welcomed into the world by wetting the newborn's lips with this sacred drink. In Igbo and Akan societies, it was believed that the spirit resident in a newborn child should have its parched throat wetted after its long journey. This ritual ensured that the spirit of the child would feel sufficiently welcome and stay, providing this celebratory drink was shared. The ritual was taken even further after a naming ceremony: the sacred liquor was not only offered to the baby again, but also to the spiritual mother, believed left in the Otherworld, so that she would not reclaim the child.

Jamaican folklore suggests that duppies, a type of ghost or spirit, are very fond of rum. It would be unconscionable not to offer them a goodly amount of rum, when courting their assistance in your endeavors. When the foundations of a new house are laid, in order to ensure a peaceful home and good fortune to the residents, rum may be sprinkled on the foundation, appeasing land and house spirits simultaneously.

Curative properties

As well as being a spiritual beverage, rum is relished for its curative properties toward body and mind. English folklore suggests that black currants

and rum will cure the most insidious colds. In fact, a splash of this elixir may stave off a cold, even before exposure. When a cold does take up residence in your body, a hot toddy has been known to work wonders: tea, honey, and rum can banish even the most resistant cold. Drinking a hot toddy while covered with a very warm blanket can create beneficial sweats, thus expelling illness. Let's also not forget rum's antiseptic and disinfectant properties — minor cuts and bruises can be cleansed with rum.

In the Caribbean, during the colonial era, rum served as a means to pay sailors and as a commodity traded in all ports. Sailors were given a weekly ration — a tot, possibly the root of "toddy" — of rum. As rum's value increased, this payment was modified by diluting rum with water and calling it grog. The sailors used rum as a

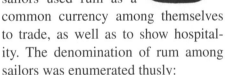

common currency among themselves to trade, as well as to show hospitality. The denomination of rum among sailors was enumerated thusly:

3 wets (a very small nip) equaled 1 sip.
3 sips equaled one gulp.
3 gulps equaled one tot.

Nelson's Blood

Rum has, on occasion, also been used to preserve the dead. A case in point: in 1805, Admiral Horatio Lord Nelson successfully engaged both the fleets of Spain and France. While bookmakers gave him horrible odds, Nelson defeated his enemies, taking seventeen ships without losing a single one of his own. Yet, as fate would have it, having received a dolorous blow, Nelson died.

In order to preserve the victorious admiral's remains during his trip back to England, his body was placed within a cask of fine rum. Nelson arrived in his homeland, pickled but intact. One might venture to say that his sailors were pickled as well, for, when the cask was opened in England, it was discovered that the rum had already been removed. Apparently, the sailors had drilled a hole into the cask during the long journey to help wet their whistles. Ever since, the term "Nelson's Blood" has been a synonym for the rum rations given to sailors.

The magical uses of rum have a long history. Given its history as a means of monetary exchange, rum can be used quite successfully in money spells. Next time you find a need to conjure up some money, offer a rum toast to your forthcoming prosperity. Court the favor of spirits with this fine drink and fine words to entreat them. Lastly, spilling some rum on the ground, while making your way through a door backwards, helps ensure that any malicious spirits stay out of your cozy home.

– DIRGEL THOMAS

Sak Yan

The sacred and magical tattoos of Thailand and Southeast Asia

THE ROOTS of tattooing are ancient and mysterious. Typically, when these primordial roots are considered, the first place that springs to mind is Polynesia, from whence the word tattoo derives. However, the art of tattooing emerged independently throughout the world, not least in Southeast Asia, where tattoos were once extremely prevalent, especially for men and where this sacred art is currently experiencing a renaissance.

Historians suggest that East Asian tattoo traditions first emerged in the China-Vietnam border regions. From here, they migrated south into what are now modern Cambodia, Laos, and Thailand, where they continued to evolve independently. Regional differences exist; however, the traditional East Asian tattoo (*sak yan*) is an indelible, fine-lined, black ink tattoo.

Yantra tattoos

Etymologists trace the word *sak* back to the proto languages of what are now southern China and northern Vietnam. *Sak* literally means "jab" or "prick" but now serves as the word for "tattoo" in Thai, Lao, and Khmer (the official language of Cambodia), as well as in other regional languages.

Yan is the Thai variant of *yantra*, a word typically translated as "sacred design" or "magical design" but which originally derives from a Pali-Sanskrit root verb meaning "to control" or "to subdue." *Sak yan* literally means "yantra tattoo."

Spiritual and Magical Roots

Sak yan derives from various spiritual and magical roots, including indigenous animism, Brahmanism, and Buddhism. Tattoos were traditionally applied by shamans or Buddhist priests. Thousands of designs exist, each intended for a specific purpose. Goals include – but are not limited to – protection, healing, mental acuity, success (financial and otherwise), and especially magical prowess.

Sak yan typically incorporate geometric designs and sacred alphabets. Khmer script is a frequent element, as many believe it to be exceptionally spiritually powerful. Images of Buddha are favored, as are images of Ganesha, Garuda, Hanuman, Vishnu, and other deities. Animal imagery is also popular.

tattoos as "raw" or unfinished. Under Western influence, however, displays of tattooed skin were considered backward and shameful. Thus, in the early 20th century, a royal decree in Chiang Mai, now the largest city in northern Thailand but once an independent kingdom, ordered women to cover their breasts and men to cover their tattoos.

Western prejudices associating tattoos with criminals also negatively affected the tradition. Communist rulers further discouraged tattoos and sak yan virtually disappeared in Communist-ruled Cambodia and Laos.

Sak yan suppressed

Sak yan was an integral component of East Asian culture for generations, but this changed in the 17th century, with the arrival of influential and judgmental Christian Europeans. By European cultural standards, tattoos were perceived as primitive. This belief was reinforced with the later arrival of Americans, especially missionaries, who vocally condemned the practice.

Local East Asian rulers were very impressed by advanced Western technology, especially military technology. The opinions of Westerners were thus given credence. Many noble and wealthy East Asian families sent their sons to study in the West. They returned home, imbued with Western ideals of beauty and Christian concepts of modesty.

In ancient days, many traditional East Asian cultures viewed men without

Temple tattoos

Sak yan persevered in Thailand, however, surviving in remote, rural areas, as well as among adherents of traditional religions. Rumors also circulated that the Thai royal family never abandoned the power and protection of sak yan.

Among those considered most responsible for preserving sak yan were wandering, indigent Buddhist monks who relied upon these magical tattoos personally for protection, spiritual and otherwise. Because of the long association with Buddhist monks, who remain among the most prominent practitioners of this ancient art, sak yan are popularly called "temple tattoos."

Angelina Jolie

Even in Thailand, sak yan appeared to be a diminishing art, until in April

2003, the tide turned, when film star and activist Angelina Jolie very publicly received her first sak yan, followed by another in 2004. Suddenly, all eyes were on sak yan. Interest was renewed within Thailand, as well as internationally.

Sak yan emerged from the mystic shadows; no longer considered primitive, but stylish and desirable instead. Once largely a man's tradition, Thai women began receiving sak yan in increasing numbers, thus further evolving the tradition.

A Living Magic Spell

Now, as in centuries past, sak yan is not mere body ornamentation. Each tattoo is a living magic spell. As with any magic spell, sak yan contains no random elements. Each and every element serves either a spiritual or a magical purpose or both.

Sak yan's power derives not only from the design, but also from the rituals involved in creation and especially from the ritualist—the tattoo artist, himself. (Sak yan masters remain virtually exclusively male.) A sak yan master is known as a *khru sak*. Each may possess a jealously guarded repertoire of designs. Many craft their own magical ink formulas. Designs and ink may also be further empowered by chanting appropriate Buddhist verses.

Masters and disciples

Various rituals are incorporated into the tattooing process. In addition, the bearer of the tattoo is not merely a canvas, but also actively influences the power and success of each sak yan. This is an interactive process. The khru sak may give the bearer of the tattoo specific magical, moral, and spiritual instructions, which must be followed to the letter, if the tattoo is expected to retain maximum power.

To receive sak yan from a specific khru sak is to effectively become that khru sak's lifelong disciple. The master must be chosen as carefully as the design. Ritual and tattoo bonds the client and the khru sak together. Depending on the specific khru sak, disciples may be encouraged to return annually to pay their respects, while recharging their sak yan.

More information and lavish illustrations may be found in *Sacred Tattoos of Thailand: Exploring the Magic, Masters, and Mysteries of Sak Yan* by Joe Cummings (Marshall Cavendish, 2011)

– JUDIKA ILLES

Celestial Fire and Blazes

The mystique and magic of the Northern Lights

FEW SIGHTS in the natural world are more unpredictable or carry more of an aura of magic and mystery than the Northern Lights, also known as the aurora borealis. Since the earliest times, the aurora borealis has both enchanted and terrified people. After all, a dazzling display shooting through the sky in shades of red, violet, and chartreuse leaves a lasting memory. Named by Galileo after Aurora, the Roman goddess of the dawn, the multi-colored shimmer of the aurora borealis covers the night sky like slow lightning bolts, boiling halos, pillars, or flowing waves.

There are also Southern Lights or the aurora australis, which appear in southern latitudes. Visible near the Antarctic from May to September, the Southern Lights can be equally impressive, but appear less frequently than their Northern counterpart.

Celestial poetry

The bright color patterns of the aurora borealis, which have been called heavenly poetry, are actually electrically charged gaseous particles in Earth's atmosphere, which collide with other particles, a solar wind, streaming from the sun. The Lights can appear at any time, when the sky is clear, but usually peak about every eleven years, just after intense sunspot cycles. Early 2014 marked the most recent peak.

The active phase of a Northern Light show generally lasts only about thirty minutes, but might repeat in two or three hours. A reddish band of afterglow may linger until dawn. The light is distributed in an oval from the magnetic poles. It is visible most often in the extreme northern latitudes, in the Arctic regions. However, the Northern Lights have been observed as far south as Texas and Louisiana and are seen periodically in Canada, Scandinavia, Siberia, and the northern United States.

Legends of the Northern Lights

Here are a few of examples of the wide variety of legends associated with the Northern Lights: the Vikings saw them as torches carried by the Valkyries illuminating the path to Valhalla. Eskimos claim that the electrical crackling noise, which sometimes accompanies the Lights, is the voices of spirits who hold torches to guide the dead to  the abyss of the afterlife. The raven is the only living creature who can join them on this journey.

The Fox tribe of Wisconsin saw the Northern Lights as an omen of war. The Lights were the ghosts of their slain enemies returning for revenge; while the Menominee, also from Wisconsin, saw great friendly giants instead, offering torches to be used for help in spearing fish. The Makah tribe of Washington State explained the Lights as a tribe of dwarves roasting whale blubber over the flames in the sky. In the Dakotas, the Mandan saw celestial medicine men brewing great kettles in which to simmer the corpses of enemies.

Distant lights

Because of Earth's curvature, the Lights can seem close enough to touch, but they actually extend up to 200 miles above the ground. They appear when the polar regions are darkest and only under a clear sky, after the heat of day has dissipated. That's why the Lights are often linked to very cold temperatures, but despite rumors to the contrary, temperature isn't really a factor in their visibility.

Labradorite, a semi-precious gem, named for Canada's Labrador Peninsula, where it is found, is a favorable stone for those who would attune to the spiritual energies of the Northern Lights. Labradorite has a midnight black matrix with swirls of pink, purple, blue, and green, as well as other colors observed in the aurora borealis. It is thought to facilitate a connection with alien worlds and the other dimensions inhabited by sky dwellers.

– ESTHER ELAYNE

The SACRED STAFF
and the
PRAYER FEATHER

THOSE WHO FOLLOW the old ways would do well to select a prayer feather carefully. Suitable choices include wild turkey (for wealth), seagull (for freedom), swan (for transformation), peacock (for vision), hawk (for journeys), and crow (for messages). Your special feather should be trimmed of any rough edges or fletchings. Next, gently stroke the feather, so that the oils in your hand can clean and straighten it, as it becomes empowered with your energy.

Make an offering to the bird, as a thank you for the feather. This can take the form of scattering bread or bird seed for food, leaving bits of string and cloth on branches for nest building materials, or even simply voicing a heartfelt "thank you." The feather is then smudged. Using a sea shell as a holder,

ignite herbs, for instance sage (for purification), cedar (for longevity), and/or lavender (for happiness). Wave the feather through the sacred herbal smoke to bless it. Talk to the feather, requesting that it serve as your own personal feather of prayer purpose.

Caring for your prayer feather

The feather can be decorated with beads, yarn — most commonly red — paint, jewelry wire wrapped with tiny crystals, and so forth. Hold the feather close to your heart to develop a rapport with it, especially when you chant, meditate, pray, or are otherwise engaged in magical workings. Care for and communicate with your feather. Use it reverently and only with good intent. The feather may be waved, drawing a healing blessing to benefit people and animal companions or to clear spaces of negative energy. The prayer feather will gradually increase in power and become an invaluable magical aid.

It is best if many others don't touch your feather. Traditionally, it is stored in its own envelope or in a bag of brown paper and kept with other medicine items, such as your rattle, shells, crystals, beads, and drum, or with the tools of the witches' art: the chalice, wand, athame, and thurible of the Craft. Upon discovering the prayer feather's wonderful potential, you may wish to add a prayer staff to your magical cupboard. This will especially appeal to witches who feel kinship with the Great Spirit of Native American magical traditions.

To make a Native American prayer staff:

Select a tree branch. The branch can be tall, like a walking staff or just the length of your hand or forearm, like a wand, according to your preference. Oak is always a good choice, as it relates to strength and endurance. Other choice sacred woods include maple (for peace and soothing), ash (for protection), elm (for honoring and mourning the dead), elder (for love), sassafras (for sweetness and pleasures), willow (to turn tears of sorrow to joy), and camphor (for healing).

The branch may be left in its natural state with the bark left on. You can also, if you prefer, strip off the bark, then sand, carve, and paint the wood, as you will, to create your staff. Tie feathers, beads, and a bell to the branch with yarn or ribbons that you find pleasing.

When it is ready, hold the staff aloft and wave it to attract the spirits. When working magic outdoors, face into the blowing wind while waving the staff. The elementals and deities will take notice. Prepare to be pleasantly surprised at how quickly they respond to your call. More sacred items and feathers can be added to the prayer staff over time. Both the prayer feather and prayer staff are versatile aids in calling in the powers to assist the witch with a variety of rituals. If treasured and treated with respect, the feather and staff will always help in times of need.

– ESTHER ELAYNE

Merry Meetings

*A candle in the window, a fire on the hearth,
a discourse over tea…*

This year *The Witches' Almanac* visits with Margot Adler, the acclaimed author, journalist, lecturer, Wiccan priestess, and correspondent for National Public Radio. Her books include *Drawing Down the Moon: Witches, Druids, Goddess-Worshippers, and Other Pagans in America Today*; *Heretic's Heart: A Journey Through Spirit and Revolution*; and *Vampires Are Us: Understanding Our Love Affair with the Immortal Dark Side*.

It has been about thirty-five years since the publication of your groundbreaking book, Drawing Down the Moon. *At that time you surveyed the personal behavior and common practices of a large portion of the personalities who comprised the Public Pagan Witchcraft movement. What were the most common affectations and personal characteristics you encountered and reported in* Drawing Down the Moon? *What stood out to you?*

Looking back, I think I wrote *Drawing Down the Moon*, partly because the Pagan and Wiccan experiences I was having in New York City were not big enough, large enough, filled with ideas. And eight times a year I would receive the *Green Egg Magazine.* And in it were some fifty pages of letters from the most interesting Pagans and Wiccans; it was intellectually so much more interesting than what I was expe-

riencing in the coven I was in.

Starhawk and I often joke that our books, *Spiral Dance* and *Drawing Down the Moon*, which came out on the same day, were both an attempt to describe the movement we wanted to exist, more than the one we were both experiencing, and lo and behold, eventually, that movement actually came to be. As for the people in the book, they, like me, were all searching for a vibrant, juicy Earth religion, that would be in harmony with the Earth and that would provide some of the same things indigenous religions provide: the songs, the stories, the sense of being a common tribe, and a relationship with the Earth that was non-exploitative, or, to be honest, less exploitative. The most amazing thing I found was how common was the experience of people encountering

Paganism for the first time: Oh, I always knew I had a religion, I just never knew its name. The feeling that it was a homecoming, something one had always known, but never had the words for.

Over the years since the publication of Drawing Down the Moon, *are there any particular individuals that you chronicled who remained on your radar and influenced you on your own personal path?*

Many people influenced me. The first thing to take me out of my very limited New York experience besides *Green Egg*, was reading *Nemeton*, which was a Pagan magazine that was written by, among others, Alison Harlow and the Pagan bard, Gwydion Pendderwen. Alison, who was trained by Victor Anderson, and was one of the original initiates into his Fairy tradition, became a close friend. Oddly we had attended the same crazy, wonderful, progressive school in Greenwich Village, although twelve years apart. This is really unusual, because there were only twenty people at most in a grade. But that school, in which I spent a whole year studying ancient Greece, and which also gave me my first May Day ceremony, is very responsible for my Pagan journey. And I would bet for Alison's too. Other people who influenced me included Selena Fox, the Zells, Harold Moss of the Church of the Eternal Source, Morgan McFarland who led a Texas Dianic group that included men, Aidan Kelly and Glenn Turner who spearheaded the NROOGD tradition, and many more.

In Drawing Down the Moon *there was a necessary focus on the who, what, and where of the movement which was clearly an important factor for you to cover. Are there any aspects of the "why we do it" which might not have been included, which you could add to the record now at this point?*

I think we have a deep need for roots. There is a saying that all of us, if we go far enough back, our ancestors were Pagan. Now, for the Irish that might only be 700 years, and for some in Eastern Europe, it might only be since the Industrial Revolution, and for Jews it might be thousands of years, but it's a real truth. And most of us Americans have been brought up in a white bread culture, without the juice of powerful traditions. Also we want those traditions in a modern context without the dogma that so often comes with them. We want to dance around a fire into the night, and still be a teacher, scientist, doctor, writer, whatever, the next morning. The Holy Rollers definitely have the juice we want; we just want it in a very modern, rationalist context. We want to be mystics and rationalists at the same time. And creating these revived traditions was one way to get there. When I lecture, one of the things I often say is that most of us in the room, who are usually mostly white, are rooting around in the ashes; we have lost both the good and the bad aspects of ancient traditions. If we are black, those traditions were destroyed by slavery. If we are Native American, most of those traditions were destroyed by colonialism, and if we are white, which most in the audience usually are, those traditions were destroyed by immigration and assimilation. Now, some of those traditions were awful. My mother,

who was brought up Jewish, was only allowed the 25 cent Hebrew teacher who taught her to say the words, while her brother was allowed the 50 cent teacher who also taught him the meaning of words. My mother was born in 1908, so this was in the teens and twenties in Brooklyn. No wonder she ran away from home at 18, worked in a factory to put herself through teacher's college, and staked out a new life filled with bohemians, the works of Alan Watts and Zen.

So we want the juice and the mystery without the dogma. We want to live in the modern world.

Pantheacon 2014 has just wrapped up and I am aware that you were an attendee. Did you find that your discoveries back in the 1970's still hold after all this time, or that the new generation of witches and Pagans have moved into new territory? By the same token have the people who you chronicled back then maintained a consistent path or do you see any significant changes?

In the last fifteen years there has been so much change. Multigenerational Pagans, Pagan chaplains, Pagan headstones at Arlington, first the pentacle, now Thor's Hammer, peer reviewed Pagan magazines, and schools with real substance like Cherry Hill. Pagans are involved seriously in interfaith, in charity events. Almost none of this was true twenty years ago. Pagans are dealing with old age, with death, and the traditions are multiplying. The whole re-constructionist field, reconstructions of Greek, Egyptian, Celtic, Druidic, Roman, Kemetic, Eastern European

Margot's reports as an NPR correspondent can be heard regularly on All Things Considered, Morning Edition *and* Weekend Edition.

religions are multiplying. People's entry into Paganism has changed. It used to be that they, like me, found a group, whatever was in the neighborhood, and there was no way to really choose, you took what you got, and later as the festival movement of the late seventies and eighties came into existence you had a chance to discover new traditions and broaden out. Now, many people come into Paganism through the internet, through festivals, or large Pagan organizations, and only later some may find a working group, coven, kindred, grove, etc. I know in my heart that had this been the situation in 1971-72 when I began my search, I would not have ended up in Wicca, but probably in Hellenic Paganism, but I knew of no groups that existed at the time.

There are loads of new young people coming into our Earth Religious movement, and one of the main topics that I found fascinating at Pantheacon this year was the question of Wiccan privilege. There are many young reconstructionists who have trouble with the word Pagan, and somehow think it stands for Wicca, which it definitely does not. Pagan is from Paganus, of the country, and in many languages it just means "the people." It is the religions not of the book, the religions that don't have prophets, that rise from the people and the Earth, and myths from thousands of years ago. It is the religions that are more tribal than creedal. Wicca is a small part of Paganism, and, quite frankly, from my perspective, not the most interesting or important part. It is Paganism as a whole that provides an ecological alternative to the religions that see humans on top and not as part of a vibrant whole, that see the Earth as just a place we are passing through, and therefore not particularly worth spending time saving. But at Pantheacon, there were many young people who spoke of feeling that Wiccans were so dominant that many ceremonies excluded them. That was something I hadn't heard before. There is also a growing division between those who see the gods as "real" and those who have more metaphoric, archetypal orientation, as I do. There are atheist and agnostic Pagans. And sometimes we are all of those things at once. I know that I can have an experience where the gods are totally real, and in another moment I see them as metaphor. I hope this division does not intensify, and that we can continue to be part of the same family. I have been to Pantheacon many times, and it is one of the best places to really see the length and breadth of Paganism. There were more than 2,300 people this time. It's also a heck of a lot of fun!

You have a new book, Vampires Are Us, *published by Weiser Books. On the Amazon.com page for the book, you are quoted, "Vampires let us play with death and the issue of mortality. They let us ponder what it would mean to be truly long lived. Would the long view allow us to see the world differently, imagine social structures differently? Would it increase or decrease our reverence for the planet? Vampires allow us to ask questions we usually bury." What is the top question that you believe should be exhumed? And what led you to write this book at this time?*

The book *Vampires Are Us* started out as a meditation on mortality as my husband was dying, but it went to very different places, and examined questions of power and identity and our relationship to the environment. It started out as a sermon, given in six mostly Unitarian churches, morphed into an essay and finally a book.

Nina Auerbach wrote, "Every age embraces the vampire it needs." Dracula was clearly an expression of England's fear of disease and immigration at a time when it had the largest ports in the world. But what were our needs, now? No one seemed to have an answer about why vampires have such traction in our culture at the moment. The major insight that came to me was that most of the popular vampires of the last thirty or more years have been conflicted, desperately struggling to be moral despite being predators, often failing in that struggle, but trying to overcome their need for blood. It's exactly who we are now, as we face a planet in threat, only our blood is oil and we are sucking the life blood out of the planet. I also realized that one of the first truly conflicted vampires was Barnabas in Dark Shadows. And while he appeared in '67, he really wasn't even called a vampire until 1968. That was the year we first saw the Earth from space, a small, blue, fragile planet that the astronauts could blot out with their thumb. We suddenly realized our vulnerability and our responsibility and moral complicity. Two years later we had the first Earth Day, our vision and views of our relationship to the Earth changed in that moment. And our vampires changed as well.

That's a tiny bit of it, but there is much more.

Astrological Alphabet Magic

Naming Familiars

IT HAS often been said that the sweetest and most welcoming of sounds is that of one's own name. Pronouncing aloud the name of another defines energy and identity. Selecting a name, whether it's for a new baby or a beloved animal companion, is a very important and serious undertaking. Names have tremendous impact on the development of personality, destiny, well-being, and overall position in the greater scheme of things.

Natal astrological indicators possess similar significance. When an animal companion is adopted, it begins a new phase of life. If its actual birthday is unknown, an astrological chart may be cast for the adoption, heralding this new cycle of life.

The letters of the alphabet are mystically linked to astrological energies and characteristics. When choosing a name for a familiar, consider the creature's horoscope, whether cast for birth or adoption. The qualities a witch wishes a familiar to develop and express may also be encouraged by careful name selection. The sounds and formation of letters create a magical energy envelope. In many ways, the birth chart and the given name become one.

Using Alphabet Magic

Consider the zodiac signs in the familiar's chart. Then look at the corresponding letter to select the initial of the name. On the following two pages are some suggestions using the letters of the English alphabet.

Alphabet Secrets

The first initial reveals the personal expression. It is the most significant influence and, in the case of a familiar, is often the only one considered. A middle or second initial shows a bridge to others. A third or final initial, the last name, describes the tribal, coven, or family dynamics.

– DIKKI-JO MULLEN

Letter	Zodiac Sign	Qualities
A	Aries	Assertive, action, pioneer, independent spirit
B	Taurus	Bountiful, beautiful, beauty, builds
C	Gemini	Cleverness, curiosity, creativity, changes
D	Cancer	Depth of feelings, determination, domestic
E	Gemini	Exclaims, expresses, evolves
F	Leo	Forceful, friendship, fun, fidelity
G	Virgo	Genius, guarded, genteel, greeter, giving
H	Capricorn/Aquarius	Heart-felt, happenings, hoarder, hider, honorable
I	Taurus/Libra	Idealist, innocent, informer, initiate, involved
J	Sagittarius	Juggler, joker, jovial, just
K	Scorpio	Keen, knave, kindred, kinetic
L	Libra	Loving, logical liberates, loyal
M	Cancer	Motherly, mingles, mindful, merciful
N	Virgo	Neatness, natural, nervous
O	Cancer/Scorpio	Obliging, opulent opinionated, operator
P	Taurus/Libra	Peaceable, pure, paradoxical, patient

Letter	Zodiac Sign	Qualities
Q	Gemini/Sagittarius	Quickest, quest, quizzical, quivering
R	Aries	Racer, rabble-rouser, release, rejuvenate, raucous, rambler
S	Capricorn	Status symbol, sentry, successful, stamina
T	Pisces	Tentative, tenderness, talents, traveler, thoroughbred
U	Sagittarius	Understands, ultimate, ultra, unifies, undaunted
V	Aquarius	Vulpine, versatility, vigilant, victorious, vistas, vitality
W	Leo	Warmth, willpower, walker, wise, witty, whimsical
X	Gemini/Pisces	Explorer, exuberant, extraordinary, X-ray
Y	Capricorn	Yearning, young-at-heart, yogi
Z	Pisces	Zest, zeal, zero, zip, zodiac, zeppelin

Umbrellas and Parasols of Shadows and Sunlight

From Buddhism to Steampunk and Voodoo ageless symbols of status and magic

UMBRELLAS and parasols — portable canopies, carried to protect against the elements — first appeared about four thousand years ago. Originally, they were held by attendants over the heads of monarchs and high priests, beings considered so sacred that they must not be touched by either rain or sunlight. From Africa to Mexico, India and the Orient, umbrellas became emblems of divine, as well as secular, power. One of the eight sacred symbols of Buddhism, the parasol's center pole represents a mountain reaching to the dome of the sky around the axis mundi, while the canopy became a solar wheel hovering over the head of Buddha. Elaborate umbrellas, displayed over Buddha's head, are actually mobile temples.

An umbrella is featured on a coin from Herod's time. In Athens, priests and priestesses of Poseidon and Athena would parade to the Acropolis beneath white umbrellas. In the Congo, umbrellas were used during marriage ceremonies to mark sacred space. A folk tale tells of a prince, who desired his brother's kingdom, demanding the royal umbrella. An historical account from nineteenth century Burma recounts how a Burmese king described himself as reigning with a great umbrella.

The Ageless Umbrella

Affectionately called a brolly, gamp, rain shade, or sunshade (UK slang), a bumbershoot (American slang), a *chattra* (Sanskrit term from India meaning mushroom), or a *parapluie* (French slang), umbrellas and parasols are collapsible structures, which encircle a single pole. The basic design is ageless, using sliding levers, similar to the umbrellas in use today. Sometimes they are large enough to stand fixed to outdoor furniture, but usually they are hand-held and carried while walking from place to place.

The word umbrella comes from the Latin *umbra*, meaning shadow or shade. This in turn derives from the Ancient Greek word *ombros*. Parasol means protection from *sol* or the sun. The words are sometimes used interchangeably, but "umbrellas" connote protection from the rain, while "parasols" suggest deflecting the hot sun. Often the clue is in the covering: an umbrella tends to be rain-

proof, while a parasol may be made of paper or light cloth. The Chinese were the first to weatherproof the covering, so parasols (protection from the sun, also symbolizing the heat of mortal suffering and desire) really predate umbrellas (protection from the rain).

Mary Poppins, gold, and feathers

During the Middle Ages, umbrellas were carried over the heads of popes, a custom still used in papal processions today. In Tibet, different deities were distinguished by their individual parasols, while Aztec rulers were shaded by parasols made of gold and feathers. The beloved parrot-headed flying umbrella, famously transported by Mary Poppins, reflects the magic, mystery, and reverence symbolized by these tools through the ages.

By the seventeenth century, parasols were becoming a familiar accessory in the civilized world, carried by ladies of all social standings. In the early nineteenth century, Jonas Handy, a popular travel writer in England, began carrying an umbrella. At first he was mocked, as this was considered feminine, but, gradually, men began to add umbrellas as essential elements in dress, both for status and practical reasons.

In 1830, the first umbrella shop, James Smith and Sons, opened in London at 53 New Oxford St. It remains in the same location today. Early European umbrellas were constructed of whale bone and wood with an oiled canvas covering. In 1852, Samuel Fox invented the first steel ribbed models, which became the forerunner of the modern compact umbrella.

Steampunk and the Second Line

Umbrellas and parasols in a myriad of colors and designs are popular both for practical use and also as collectibles today. At Disney World, personalized umbrellas are offered for sale with the purchaser's names painted on, upon request. As promotional giveaways, decorated umbrellas are frequently offered as prizes by newspapers and other businesses. Steampunk aficionados and others who don historical dress often add a touch of authenticity and magic by selecting a special umbrella or parasol to complete their costumes.

In New Orleans, black umbrellas, along with a handkerchief and top hat, are essential accessories at jazz funeral processions. Opening the umbrella symbolizes the release of the soul to the afterlife. In Voodoo, the umbrella becomes a sort of magic wand, carried to invoke the powerful spirit, Baron Samedi, Master of the Cemetery. Pointed at a target, it might be spun clockwise to offer a blessing or turned rapidly counterclockwise to invoke a more sinister energy.

– ELAINE NEUMEIER

The Honorable Olivia Melian Durdin-Robertson

Pagan Priestess and Founder of the Fellowship of Isis

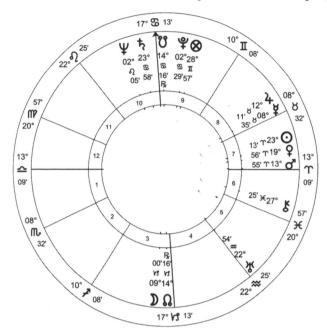

"IT WAS ON A Friday the 13th," the Honorable Olivia Melian Durdin-Robertson often said gleefully, with a subtle nod, when mentioning her birthday. Known as Lady Olivia to her thousands of followers around the world, she was among the most influential and admired Pagan priestesses of modern times.

Born during World War 1, on April 13, 1917, at 6:50 PM BST in St. Mary's Hospital in London, Lady Olivia seemed destined to live the life of a mystic, writer, bohemian, and artist. Her parents, Nora and Manning Durdin-Robertson, were close friends of the poet W. B. Yeats. Robert Graves, author of *The White Goddess*, was her cousin. In 1925 the family moved from London to Ireland upon inheriting the ancestral home at the death of her grandmother.

Olivia's Capricorn Moon describes a childhood connection to the past as well as an affinity for nature. Early photographs show her riding horses with her brother. The cover photo of the book *Clonegal Castle* portrays Olivia outdoors holding a favorite white cat. It was well known that the castle always had white cats. Her Moon was in the 3rd house, conjoining the North Node. This shows her deep attachment to her supportive older brother, Reverend Lawrence Durdin-Robertson, who, along with his wife Pamela, greatly assisted Olivia in her endeavors. The Disseminating Moon phase indicates an inherent gift for teaching and sharing her experiences to benefit others.

Her Mercury-Jupiter conjunction in Taurus indicates that she was well educated, attending the Heathfield School in Ascot and the Grosvenor School of Art. The 8th house placement of the Taurus planets showed her financial good fortune of being supported through her family's inheritance. Olivia's Part of Fortune and Pluto were in her 9th house, indicating ability in advanced scholarship and potential as an author. She completed her formal education in 1942, graduating from University College in Dublin. The first of Olivia's many books, *St. Malachy's Court*, was published in 1946. Among her later works one, *Field of the Stranger*, was given the London Book Society's Choice Award in 1948. She had two public art exhibitions and illustrated her own books. Later, her love of art was expressed in creating various altars and paintings, which were rich in astrological and goddess symbolism. Uranus in Aquarius in the 5th house points to her originality and great creativity.

Her Libra ascendant, ruled by Venus, and her stellium in Aries with Venus, Mars, and the Sun, reveal her personal charisma, beauty, and her great artistry. Even in old age Olivia was striking in appearance, beautifully dressed in colorful robes and capes. She was agile in movement well into her nineties, petite with long, flowing hair. True to the pioneering spirit of Aries, Lady Olivia

spurred the goddess movement by establishing the Fellowship of Isis, an international spiritual group dedicated to promoting the divine feminine through honoring the Egyptian goddess Isis. Despite her strong 7th house, there is no record that she ever married; however, she was always hospitable, ready to share her life with others and participate in team projects.

As early as 1960 Lady Olivia and Rev. Lawrence had established a local welfare system and a center at Clonegal (Huntington) Castle for service, meditation, and study. In the true Yeatsian tradition they prepared to welcome the Aquarian Age. In 1975 – 1976 Lady Olivia wrote her spiritual autobiography, *The Call of Isis*, at the time of her second Saturn return. This was when she formally established the Fellowship of Isis. Her natal Saturn was in Cancer, powerfully positioned in the 10th house, along with her natal Neptune in Leo. Those placements indicated her work being done at her home, while also having a universal impact.

Lady Olivia passed away peacefully in her sleep, surrounded by her family, on the evening of November 14, 2013, in Wexford, Ireland at the age of 96. The transiting Moon and Uranus were in Aries and transiting Pluto and Venus (Venus ruled her natal 8th house of death as well as her ascendant) were in Capricorn, exactly conjunct her natal Moon at the time of her passing. This hints that the gate to the Summerland was standing open, ready to welcome a great soul, Lady Olivia, to a new plane of existence. She left behind these gracious words embodying the wisdom of her spiritual path:

Be happy now. Don't worry about if you were happy yesterday or whether you will be happy tomorrow. Eternity is between seconds. You find Deity, the Goddess, the God, now. And your home becomes your sanctuary as your hearth–a candle, one candle, a stick of incense, wherever you are is Heaven. That's what my message is – yes – wherever you are should be Heaven.

Video clips featuring interviews with Lady Olivia and more information about her work can be found at http://www.fellowshipofisis.com.

– Dikki-Jo Mullen

Olivia Melian Durdin-Robertson

Olivia Melian Durdin-Robertson was born Friday, April 13, 1917, at 6:50 PM BST in London, England

Data Table
Tropical Placidus

Sun 23 Aries 13 – 7th house

Moon 09 Capricorn 00 – 3rd house
(waning Moon in the Disseminating phase)

Mercury 08 Taurus 35 – 8th house

Venus 19 Aries 56 – 7th house

Mars 13 Aries 55 – 7th house

Jupiter 12 Taurus 11 – 8th house

Saturn 23 Cancer 58 – 10th house

Uranus 22 Aquarius 54 – 5th house

Neptune 02 Leo 05 – 10th house

Pluto 02 Cancer 29 – 9th house

Chiron 27 Pisces 25 – 6th House

N. Moon Node 14 Capricorn 16 – 3rd house

Part of Fortune 28 Gemini 57 – 9th house

Ascendant (rising sign) is 13 Libra 09

Gourds

A first and great gift from Mother Nature

EACH AUTUMN, their mysterious presence lends a supernatural aura to farmers markets and grocery store produce sections. They appear, often heaped among the new harvest of apples and potatoes or perhaps near their relatives, the melons, squashes, and pumpkins. Almost like snowflakes, each gourd seems to be truly unique. Twisted into bizarre shapes, both mocking and resembling birds, fish, snakes, gnomes, and other creatures; striped and mottled in colors ranging from white to green, brown, orange, yellow, even black, purple, and maroon; often covered in warty growths; gourds have a perennial appeal.

Some are tiny, resembling berries. Others are huge. Visitors to Clemons Produce Market in Orlando, Florida can marvel at a permanent display of four "long gourds." Suspended along one wall, they are each about 10 feet long and resemble beige-colored serpents.

An ancient crop

Gourds are among the most ancient plants. Unsavory in flavor and scant in flesh, they are mostly inedible. Yet, ironically, they were the first crop to be domesticated throughout the ancient world and continue to be popular choices for home gardens and commercial farms today.

Gourds have been grown for many thousands of years; cherished first for making utensils, then as musical instruments and decorations. Research shows that they were the only crop to have been used by all known early cultures in the temperate and tropical climate zones. The fruit's hard rind or shell is remarkably strong and versatile when dried and cut or carved. Gourds were fashioned into containers long before baskets or pottery was invented.

Cups and canteens

Very early examples come from Peru, where seeds and fragments of gourd shell were dated to 10,000 BCE by archaeologists. In Mexico, gourd fragments dating to 7,000 BCE have been found. Excavations of

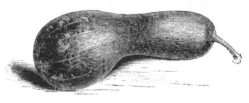

Native American sites near Gainesville, Florida date gourd use to 11,000 BCE. By the 3rd century BCE, gourds were familiar in Greece, mentioned by Hippocrates as being used as cups. It has long been noted that gourds make perfect canteens. Their porous skin acts like a refrigerator, allowing outer condensation to evaporate, therefore keeping the drink inside fresh and cool.

As society evolved, so did the use of gourds. The hard outer shell has been found surrounded with a silver top and bottom, making an elegant cup for sipping maté tea in the Andes. Gourd rattles with the dried seeds inside have long been used as rhythm instruments. They have been fashioned into mandolins and guitars, as well. Bird houses are another long time popular use.

Magical workings

Today, gourd art sold at Native American Pow Wows and art galleries is beautifully painted with mystical designs, decorated with wood burning, crystals, and sea shells. At Halloween, artists offer jack o' lanterns, fashioned from round gourds painted bright orange, carved with a traditional smile, and lit from within by a tiny battery operated candle. Larger gourds, which stand upright, have been turned into portable altars. A hole is cut in the side and a seashell holding sage for burning placed within. Other clever gourd art offers a new twist on the dream catcher in creating a base for the web.

During the harvest and autumn holiday celebrations, merely placing a selection of gourds on the altar or dinner table is a beautiful and inexpensive way to evoke the mood and merriment of the season. Think about the ongoing traditions behind gourds and their importance since earliest times. As your own gourds dry, perhaps you can find an original way to use them in your own magical workings. Garden witches living in Zone 7 and further south can just toss the seeds out and watch for the gourds to appear in different and fascinating shapes next year. Plant enthusiasts in northern climates must enjoy them as house plants.

A number of organizations, in several states and internationally, exist for those who wish to explore the possibilities gourds offer further. For example, the American Society of Gourd Artists at Americangourdsociety.org is an excellent resource.

– MOTHER OLLMANN

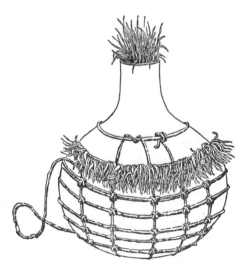

Our Mothers Who Eat

Witches and the Divine Feminine

THE YORUBA OF southwestern Nigeria have long honored a pantheon of deities (*Orisa*) and spirits that often convey a complex understanding of the world, its beginnings, and their place in the cosmos. Of these deities and spirits, the singular most complex of these energies is the divine feminine as embodied in the Spirit of the Witches.

The Yoruba pantheon is seemingly patrifocal; however, the feminine divine occupies a prominent place in a less than overt manner. On the surface, one would assume the ascendancy of masculine power both in divine and mundane planes. It is the adjudicating Orisa Esu, Orunmila, and Obatala who occupy primary cosmological positions as protagonist, destiny, and purity respectively. However, it is via female divinity that all of these powers are conveyed through to the corners of the cosmos and into the world of mankind.

There is a collective energy known as *Aje* that pervades all female Orisa. This energy is so powerful and mysterious that it rarely spoken of in less than a reverent (and cautious) manner. Aje is understood to mean the "witch power," the primal power that vivifies the universe with the power to grant existence out of nothingness or in an instant return the something into the nothingness. This rarefied energy strikes fear into all males, be it Orisa or man.

Sacred purposes and powers

How did this awesome energy that is all powerful come into being? In the beginnings of time, the first energies to emanate from the high god Olodumare were all male energies, save the one female being. In its fullness of universal understanding, Olodumare knew that there must be a balance to the universe and this female being was endowed with a power that exceeded each singular male being and in some ways their sum.

As these energies journeyed forth from the center of creation, it was the female energy alone that returned to the Creator, asking for a purpose. She queried Olodumare on what it was that she bore into the universe and into the world. She exhorted that some of the Orisa had the ability to create victory, some had the ability to create fire, some had the ability to build, and others had the ability to create roads into the wilderness, but she had no special purpose.

Special energy

Olodumare thought about this and to the single female creation that he wrought, he gave the power of the word and the power of birth and death. Olodumare gave her the bird as her symbol and the calabash to contain her power. The high god explained to her that she was the mother of all, able to give life and to take life.

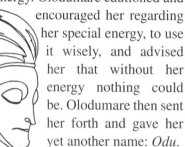

Olodumare furthered that only through her could all of Olodumare's creations know the word of the Creator. Hers was indeed a mystical power that was balance to the expansive qualities of male energy. Olodumare cautioned and encouraged her regarding her special energy, to use it wisely, and advised her that without her energy nothing could be. Olodumare then sent her forth and gave her yet another name: *Odu.*

To fully understand the implications of this awesome energy that Olodumare sent into the universe, it is necessary to understand her many names and appellations. Her primary name, Aje, is a contraction of two words, *iya je*, roughly translating as *mother eats.* The Mother Eats, on the surface, refers to Aje's ability to eat away at the very life that she gives. On a deeper level, it is Aje that eats of the energy of the very Creator that vivifies the universe and spews life out of her calabash.

The Calabash of Existence

The calabash, the container of the Aje's power, is none other than the womb of the Creator. In this sacred calabash is the material of existence itself. This primordial calabash contains the holy elements which create life in the mind of the Yoruba. It contains the essences that embody all existence, the colors red, white, and black. Every element of the known universe is said to spring from one of these classifying elements or a combination of these elements. In fact, the calabash is often referred to as the Calabash of Existence.

The male forces that emanated from Olodumare are expansive. Without the restriction of the Sacred Calabash, they would fly apart and dissipate. It is through the Calabash of Existence that the expansive force of the creation is harnessed and given form. Dynamic energy must be tied up in form to give it purpose. It is in this capacity that Aje is given yet another appellation: the Sustainer of Existence. While the male generative force comes in a flash, it is the female nurturing energy that sustains the created, both as gestation and later as nurturer.

In the physical body of women, the natural extension of the divine female energy is the secret of life. Receptive of the male expansive energies, a woman's womb, like the Calabash of Existence, is the space in which life is secreted. It is a microcosm of the macrocosm, who like the Aje, provide the sole ability to gestate life.

Female Divine

Another name for Aje is *Odu*. This word of mysterious origin has many meanings, all of which are tied up in the being of the creator Olodumare. Odu is not only a female emanation of Olodumare; Odu is also the sacred utterance of Olodumare through which the universe sprung into existence. In this coded enigmatic language, the universe is expressed in the sixteen primary utterances of the Creator. These sixteen utterances combined to create 256 expressions of the divine. Aje, under the name Odu, is directly related to Creation itself and the Creator. As the repository of the expressions of the Creator, Odu participates in creation and the myriad of possibilities, as the mystical substrate.

While the many blessings of Aje have been outlined, the feminine divine is also seen as a dispenser of justice for those that have broken the natural order of Olodumare. Those that dare break the laws of divine order suffer the plague of the birds of Aje that tear at the very being of the offender. They are said to infest the dreams of the offenders and feed on their liver and intestines. Incited, the Aje will mete out justice by un-creating the transgressor, be they Orisa or human.

Mothers of All

How is this divine force conveyed into the world of humans? The divine energy of Iyami move into the world of existence in the personage of women and all female animals, as extensions of the "power" of the divine feminine. In everyday life, the Yoruba will not directly speak the name Aje, instead they will refer to this complex energy as *Iyami* ("our mothers"), in order to avoid bringing on unwanted attention or perchance offending this awesome power.

In the highly patriarchal society of the Yoruba, women are honored as the mothers of all, who, like the Iyami, can bring life, peace, and many blessings. Because women directly participate in the divinity of Iyami, crossing them is believed to bring drought, sterility, war, and illness.

Fathers and Mothers of Ifa

Women's deep mystical energy is in-born, as opposed to man who must be initiated to attain the same mystical vision. As an example, the primary cult of Yoruba society is Ifa and their male priests are known as Babalawo (Father of Secrets), with adjunct female priestesses known as Iyanifa (Mother of Ifa). During the initiation of a babalawo, the initiate is presented to the sacred Calabash of Existence, where Odu power is, in order that they might receive the power of the word (*ofo ase*). Men can only develop this power through this exposition to Odu. Women, however are not presented to Odu, since they are born with the qualities of *ofo ase* and Odu is resident in their own Calabash of the Existence: their wombs.

In the ultimate paradox, it is the babalawo who is seen as senior to the iyanifa. In the cult of Ifa, the Calabash of Existence must be present for an initiation, whether it is for a babalawo or an iyanifa. While a babalawo may have and view the interior of the Calabash, a woman may not, because it is believed that such a concentration of energy (the combination of her own and that of the calabash) would instantly kill her or drive her mad.

Mysteries of Odu

Another example of the subtext of power Iyami and women is found in the secular society. The Yoruba have a long tradition of feudal kings. The installation of a king is often performed by an older woman or his mother. During the coronation, the king is crowned with a beaded conical crown that contains the very mysteries of Odu, the Calabash of Existence, and symbols of Iyami. Inside the crown of almost every king is a Calabash of Existence and the apex of the exterior of the crown is the very bird of the Iyami. The calabash assures that the king rules with the very utterances of Olodumare crowning him and the bird acts as the mediator between the banality of the earth and the divinity

of heaven. When, in the rare instance, a female is crowned as monarch, the crown does not contain the Calabash.

Crafty Women

To the ordinary man, Aje is understood as a persona (a witch), as well as the subtext of being that is an energy which animates the divine feminine. Crafty women, who display acute awareness and/or luck are often referred to as Iyami and, in the rare instance where they dare aspirate the word, Aje. The ancient Yoruba had a special understanding of the power of women, and while they had a uniquely patrilineal thrust, they understood that certain duties were strictly under the purview of women, like the control of the money as the merchants of the markets. In the same sacred poetry of Osa Meji, society is advised to respect women for their prowess and ability to convey power, be it secular or spiritual.

In the modern world, the understanding of Iyami has devolved from an understanding of the divine participation of the feminine into one of fear of feminine power. There is a pervasive fear of women's ability to obstruct rather than understand the *ofo ase* that they naturally carry. Despite the fear that surrounds the capabilities of women, they are culturally indispensable. It is women who gives us birth; it is women who control the market place; it is women who crown kings who wear the symbol of their birds on top of their crowns. All men are dependent on women for their existence, whether they are kings who rule by consent of the Iyami or common men.

– Ifadoyin Sangomuyiwa

Excerpt from Osa Meji regarding Iyami

Olodumare said, what is your power?

It said, for all of time you will be called their mother

It said, because when you departed, the three of you together,

It said, you, the only woman among them, returned

It said, to this woman is given the Power

Which makes you their mother

It said, you, you will uphold the world

Olodumare itself gives you the Power

When Olodumare gives you the Power,
it gives you the Power of the bird

It is Olodumare who brings the Power of Eleye,
the owner of the bird

When Olodumare brought forth the Power of Eleye,
Olodumare said it is good

Olodumare said, this Eleye Calabash,
which it had brought into being

Olodumare said, do you know its use in the World?

Olodumare said, you will know its use in the word

Odu said, she will know it

She received the bird from Olodumare

She then received the Power that she would use with it

She departed

The Galactic Center

The Sun of our Sun — a fixed star essence in the Milky Way

SINCE 2008 *The Witches' Almanac* has featured a different fixed star each year. One of astrology's earliest traditions, the influences of the fixed stars were analyzed by dedicated astrologers around the ancient world. The stars were charted long before the houses, aspects, and signs of the zodiac were established. Each is an individual sun, radiating its own energy field to emit a unique celestial power, which can significantly impact earthly matters.

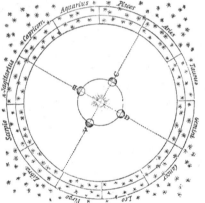

This year's choice is different. It departs from the ancient catalogue of stars in order to feature the work of a contemporary scientist, Karl Jansky. The idea is to explore a perspective on the phenomenon of fixed stars from the inside out.

Jansky made his discovery in 1932. While researching the source of atmospheric disturbances, which interfered with the reception on telephone lines, he determined that the center of our galaxy, the Galactic Center of the Milky Way, was a point of significant influence. The Galactic Center was recognized as a place of immense energy. It is a huge black hole and actually contains the collapsed mass of millions of stars. The Galactic Center is the gravitational center around which our own sun orbits. The galaxy's nucleus is 26,000 light years from Earth. It revolves at about 135 miles a second and its 225 million year orbit period is called the cosmic year.

Currently, the Galactic Center is located at 27 degrees of Sagittarius. Like the fixed stars, it shifts slowly, taking about 72 years to move a single zodiacal degree. Since the 1960s, astrologers have placed the Galactic Center in individual horoscopes. It is read as a sensitive point, much like the lunar nodes or Part of Fortune might be, but it ushers in an otherworldly or multi-dimensional quality. To understand exactly what this means to you on a personal level, check your own horoscope to see the house placement for 27 degrees of Sagittarius, as well as any planets within three degrees.

In an individual's birth chart, the Galactic Center shows where travel, education, moral discussions, and spirituality come into play. A knowledge of higher consciousness, foreign places, even including extraterrestrial civilizations, have been linked to it. The equilibrium of the personality, highest aspirations, and the influence an individual might have on the environment are revealed by its position. Contemporary research shows that the intense energy generated by the black hole at the Galactic Center is intercepted by our own solar system. It is distributed by the pattern of the planets at a given moment. A good analogy is to think of it as radio signals interpreted in a specific way according to the shape of a specific antenna.

Both the planetary placements at birth, as well as the transiting planets in astrology forecasts, can be clarified by considering the Galactic Center. An orb of three degrees works well for the purpose of interpretation. Those born from December 17–22 of any year will have the Sun conjunct the Galactic Center.

In the year to come, Mercury will transit the Galactic Center from December 6–11, 2015. This can affect travel plans, educational opportunities, and communication with animals. Venus will transit there from January 20–25, 2016. Important decisions

regarding love as well as creative breakthroughs will be possible. Celebrity romances and artistic endeavors can be in the news. Looking further ahead, Saturn will conjoin the Galactic Center February–December 2017. This time period promises some profound situations, perhaps bringing about the development of a new religion as well as shifting allegiances between governments around the world.

Perhaps the Sabian Symbol for this degree of the zodiac offers a further clue concerning the promise of the Galactic Center. It reads, "An old bridge over a beautiful stream." "Conservation" is the keyword for the degree of this Sabian Symbol. It suggests dependability and honoring the underlying need to preserve enduring structures.

If the horoscope overall is a prominent one, then a prominent placement of the Galactic Center at birth can indicate an exceptional life mission or abilities. Steven Spielberg's Sun and Thomas Edison's Moon were conjunct the Galactic Center at birth. So are the ascendants (rising signs) of Prince William, Oprah, Mother Theresa, Sylvester Stallone, Catherine Zeta Jones, and Pierce Brosnan.

– DIKKI-JO MULLEN

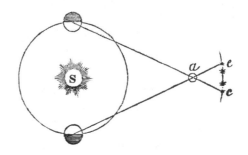

TAROT BIRTHDAY CORRESPONDENCES

I REGULARLY run into people who have read these ubiquitous, dime-a-dozen birthday/astrology books that one typically finds in the bargain bins of large, corporate bookstores. You know the kind — big, colorful, hardcover varieties with tons of pretty pictures and cluttered lay-outs. Nothing one would deem scholarly, per se, but certainly worthy of a place on the coffee table; that is, if your coffee table happened to be located at Madam Mafalda's Discount Psychic Emporium. (Free smudge stick with every aura cleansing purchase!) When the topic of tarot cards pops up in the conversation, they are wonderfully quick to say, "My birthday card is The Lovers," or something of the sort, referencing the book in question. I have rarely found the correspondence to make sense.

Therefore, I decided to write this little ditty about how to determine the tarot card(s) associated with one's birthday for the general reader. Those of you who are particularly well-versed in tarot, astrology, or Qabalah have probably heard this information a few dozen times already. However, for those who have not yet immersed themselves in this proverbial pool of knowledge, we shall begin as simply as possible.

The Major Arcana

The Major Arcana of the tarot are all of those cards with the big, fancy titles. The Emperor, Death, The Tower, The Sun, Temperance, etc., all fall into this category. There are 22 Major Arcana cards and each one corresponds either to an element, a planet, or a zodiac sign. It will be the zodiac signs that we will pay particularly close attention to, at first. My zodiac sign, for example, is Leo, which corresponds to the Major Arcana card entitled Strength in most decks (although other decks might call it something different, like Lust or Fortitude). For the first card corresponding to your birthday, simply check out the list below.

Aries – The Emperor
Taurus – The Hierophant
Gemini – The Lovers
Cancer – The Chariot
Leo – Strength
Virgo – The Hermit

Libra – Justice
Scorpio – Death
Sagittarius – Temperance
Capricorn – The Devil
Aquarius – The Star
Pisces – The Moon

Simple enough. Step one is completed. Step two is where things get a little more specific and tricky.

The Minor Arcana

All of the cards that are assigned numbers and objects, such as the 4 of Pentacles or the 6 of Cups, fall beneath the banner of the Minor Arcana. Occultists and astrologers will regularly reference the influence of the four elements — fire, water, air, and earth. As you may have noticed, there are four different suits found in the Minor Arcana. As such, they correspond to the four elements as follows:

Fire – Wands
Water – Cups
Air – Swords
Earth – Pentacles
    (known as Disks or Coins in certain tarot decks)

Each zodiac sign also falls into one of the elemental categories:

Fire – Wand: Aries, Leo, Sagittarius
Water – Cups: Cancer, Scorpio, Pisces

Air – Swords: Libra, Aquarius, Gemini
Earth – Pentacle: Capricorn, Taurus, Virgo

Astrology places the signs in each elemental category under an

additional heading: either cardinal, fixed, or mutable. What each term means is not particularly important for our purposes. However, you might want to check the handy guide below to see where your zodiac sign falls.

Aries – Cardinal Fire
Leo – Fixed Fire
Sagittarius – Mutable Fire
Cancer – Cardinal Water
Scorpio – Fixed Water
Pisces – Mutable Water
Libra – Cardinal Air
Aquarius – Fixed Air
Gemini – Mutable Air
Capricorn – Cardinal Earth
Taurus – Fixed Earth
Virgo – Mutable Earth

A long time ago, some clever old coot decided to also correspond each of the zodiac signs to cards in the Minor Arcana. The Aces were not included in this scheme. Therefore, every 2, 3, and 4 corresponds to a cardinal zodiac sign; every 5, 6, and 7 to a fixed sign; and every 8, 9, and 10 to a mutable sign.

You may have heard the zodiac referred to as a wheel. Anyone who has glimpsed at an astrological chart might have noticed it seeming rather circular and wheel-like. (Warning: Basic math to follow. Do not be alarmed.)

As your old geometry teacher told you, there are 360 degrees in a circle, meaning that each zodiac sign takes up 30 degrees of space ($360/12 = 30$) on the astrological wheel. However, astrologers were not yet content and decided to split up each zodiac sign into three additional divisions known as "decans" (10 degree increments).

Aries

2 (Mar 21 to Mar 30), 3 (Mar 31 to Apr 10) 4 (Apr 11 to Apr 20) of Wands

Leo

5 (July 22 to Aug 1), 6 (Aug 2 to Aug 11), 7 (Aug 12 to Aug 22) of Wands

Sagittarius

8 (Nov 23 to Dec 2), 9 (Dec 3 to Dec 12), 10 (Dec 13 to Dec 21) of Wands

Cancer

2 (June 21 to July 1), 3 (July 2 to July 11), 4 (July 12 to July 21) of Cups

Scorpio

5 (Oct 23 to Nov 1), 6 (Nov 2 to Nov 12), 7 (Nov 13 to Nov 22) of Cups

Pisces

8 (Feb 19 to Feb 28), 9 (Mar 1 to Mar 10), 10 (Mar 11 to Mar 20) of Cups

Libra

2 (Sept 23 to Oct 2), 3 (Oct 3 to Oct 12), 4 (Oct. 13 to Oct. 22) of Swords

Aquarius

5 (Jan 20 to Jan 29), 6 (Jan 30 to Feb 8), 7 (Feb 9 to Feb 18) of Swords

Gemini

8 (May 21 to May 31), 9 (June 1 to June 10), 10 (June 11 to June 20) of Swords

Capricorn

2 (Dec 22 to Dec 30), 3 (Dec 31 to Jan 9), 4 (Jan 10 to Jan 19) of Pentacles

Taurus

5 (Apr 21 to Apr 30), 6 (May 1 to May 10), 7 (May 11 to May 20) of Pentacles

Virgo

8 (Aug 23 to Sept 1), 9 (Sept 2 to Sept 11), 10 (Sept 12 to Sept 22) of Pentacles

The first decan represents the first 10 degrees of a sign, second decan degrees 11-20, and the third degrees 21-30. As you may have guessed, these decans subsequently correspond to tarot cards. So, the first decan of the cardinal sign Aries corresponds to the 2 of Wands, the second decan to the 3 of Wands, etc. In the case of zodiac signs, you don't need an astrological chart to figure out your degree, just refer to the handy-dandy chart at the top of this page.

Since my birthday is August 15, which falls within the third decan of the Leo cycle, the Minor Arcana card associated with my birthday is the 7 of Wands. I now have two cards connected to my birthday: Strength and the 7 of Wands.

Court Cards

Also nestled within the Minor Arcana are things referred to as "court cards." These are the Kings, Queens, Knights, Pages, Princes, etc. There are usually four sets of four court cards (one set of four for each suit) in a tarot deck. As you might have guessed, these also correspond to a section of the astrological wheel, although the placements are not nearly as neat and tidy.

The Pages (known as Princesses or Knaves in some decks) are not factored into this equation. However, the Kings, Queens, and Knights are more than willing to step up to the plate.

(Note: Tarot decks tend to vary quite a bit here. Though Queens tend to remain Queens across the board, Knights, Kings, and Princes tend to switch places depending upon the deck in question. The list below corresponds to more traditional decks like the Rider Waite, Visconti-Sforza, or Marseilles. If using the Thoth deck, Knights should replace Kings and Princes should replace Knights. Other decks will occasionally do something similar.)

Therefore, the three cards associated with my birthday would be Strength, the 7 of Wands, and the King of Pentacles. Now then, with what you have just learned, which tarot cards would be associated with your birthday?

—DIKKI -JO MULLEN

King of Wands
November 13 to December 12 – 20° Scorpio to 20° Sagittarius

Queen of Wands
March 11 to April 10 – 20° Pisces to 20° Aries

Knight of Wands
July 12 to August 11 – 20° Cancer to 20° Leo

King of Cups
February 9 to March 10 – 20° Aquarius to 20° Pisces

Queen of Cups
June 11 to July 11 – 20° Gemini to 20° Cancer

Knight of Cups
October 13 to November 12 – 20° Libra to 20° Scorpio

King of Swords
May 11 to June 10 – 20° Taurus to 20° Gemini

Queen of Swords
September 12 to October 12 – 20° Virgo to 20° Libra

Knight of Swords
January 10 to February 8 – 20° Capricorn to 20° Aquarius

King of Pentacles
August 12 to September 11 – 20° Leo to 20° Virgo

Queen of Pentacles
December 13 to January 9 – 20° Sagittarius to 20° Capricorn

Knight of Pentacles
April 11 to May 10 – 20° Aries to 20° Taurus

The Lesser Banishing Ritual of the Pentagram

MANY CONSIDER the Lesser Banishing Ritual of the Pentagram (LBRP for short) as the cornerstone of the Golden Dawn tradition of High Ritual Magic. The Hermetic Order of the Golden Dawn is a mystical order, founded in 1888 by three British Freemasons: S. L. MacGregor Mathers, William Wynn Westcott and William Robert Woodman. Before the order disbanded in 1900, splintering into multiple and distinct organizations, its members included such luminaries as Irish poet W. B. Yeats, authors A. E. Waite and Dion Fortune, and occultist Aleister Crowley, the so-called "wickedest man in the world."

Although, in practice, the LBRP is a relatively simple ritual, it incorporates within its structure many layers of complex symbolism. It is used primarily to banish unwanted negative influences, but also has a multitude of other uses, such as centering oneself, expanding one's aura, aligning oneself to the energies of the sun and clearing temple space before and after evocation rituals. According to Crowley, "Those who regard this ritual as a mere device to invoke or banish spirits are unworthy to possess it. Properly understood, it is the Medicine of Metals and the Stone of the Wise." The aspiring magician would do well, then, to study, learn and memorize the LBRP.

Before we discuss the "script and blocking" of the ritual, a few correspondences must be established:

Most magical rituals begin in the east. Even when they do not, the temple or ritual space used is almost always oriented toward the east—the direction of the rising sun. That being said, the elemental attributions of the four directions are as follows:

East – Air
South – Fire
West – Water
North – Earth

It has been said that the Golden Dawn's Hermetic magic deals mostly with the "Solar" current — i.e. the forces or energies surrounding the Sun. When you perform the LBRP, one begins in the east, where the Sun rises, and then travels deosil (clockwise), in the same way that the Sun moves throughout the sky. Also, the God-names vibrated at each quarter specifically correspond to the Sun's orientation, rather than the elements found at each quarter.

East – Dawn – YHVH (*Yud-Heh-Vav-Heh*): The name of God signifying the mystery of creation.

South – Noon – Adonai: "The Lord", the Sun at its zenith.

West – Sunset – Eheieh: "I am that I am/will be", the setting Sun, hinting at resurrection.

North – Night – AGLA (*Ah-Gu-Lah*): Short for "Atah Gibor Le'ohlam Adonai" or "Thou art mighty forever, my Lord." A blessing to the Sun as it "travels in darkness."

Four mighty archangels are evoked during the LBRP or at the very least their essences will be present, when called upon. Each of these archangels rules a direction, as well as the element associated with that direction:

Raphael – East – Air

Michael – South – Fire

Gabriel – West – Water

Uriel – North – Earth

According to this system, each element is assigned a specific color, as well:

Yellow – Air – Raphael

Red – Fire – Michael

Blue – Water – Gabriel

Black – Earth – Uriel

When visualizing the archangels, each holds a "weapon" of sorts. These are as follows:

Raphael — caduceus wand of wisdom

Michael — flaming sword of righteousness

Gabriel — the Holy Graal chalice

Uriel — the disk or pentacle, which may serve as a shield

Those familiar with certain styles of reading tarot may find this confusing, because of potential conflicting correspondences associated with similar ritual implements. In some tarot traditions, wands are associated with fire, while swords are associated with the element of air. It should be noted, that those are not the traditional implements of the two archangels in question for specific reasons:

Wands are associated with fire in the tarot, because of their correspondence to the Qabalistic world of Atziluth. In this regard, fire is seen not as the combustion of materials, but as the initial spark of life that animates and inspires all living things. It is passion in the truest, most primal sense and is therefore unrefined. Torches and kindling come to mind.

The wand held by Archangel Raphael, however, is the caduceus most associated with Hermes-Mercury, known as the divine physician. The name Raphael may be translated literally as "God heals." Air, the element governed by Raphael, rules the intellect and the caduceus is viewed as an implement of wisdom. One should also note that in certain grimoires, most notably the Heptameron, Raphael is associated with the planet Mercury.

Similarly, the tarot swords are implements of the intellect. Although in many cases used for war (a fiery, martial endeavor), the creation of a sword takes knowledge, skill, artfulness, and metallurgical prowess honed by years of instruction. In contrast, the sword of Archangel Michael is not constructed from steel, but is an implement of pure, celestial flame. So, when we completely combine these correspondences, we are left with:

East – Air – Yellow – Raphael – Caduceus – Dawn – YHVH

South – Fire – Red – Michael – Flaming Sword – Noon – Adonai

West – Water – Blue – Gabriel – Chalice – Sunset – Eheieh

North – Earth – Black – Uriel – Pentacle – Evening – AGLA

Now then, there is the necessary "drawing of the banishing earth pentagram" found at each direction of this ritual. A standard pentagram is drawn in the air with either a finger or a consecrated dagger — I personally prefer a finger. To draw the banishing earth pentagram (see figure on page XX), you would begin at the bottom left point of the pentagram and travel up and center, to the top center point.

To further clarify, if I use my right hand to draw the pentagram, I begin with my right arm across my body, finger pointing down, toward a point past my left hip, and then draw a line up and toward the center, so that the next point is above the middle of my forehead, followed by a downward line past my right hip, and so forth, until, finally, we are back where we started and have visualized a bright, flaming deep blue pentagram.

The pentagrams are connected with a bright, flaming red "line" that, when complete and hypothetically viewed as if from above, forms a circle. The colors blue and red correspond directly to the Tree of Life Sephiroth of Chesed (Mercy) and Geburah (Might), respectively. Another name

for Chesed is Gedulah (see the Qabalistic Cross section of the ritual). The balancing point of these two Sephiroth is Tiphareth (Beauty), considered to be the sphere of the Sun, as well as the sixth Sephirah on the Tree of Life (see the mention of "the six-rayed star" in the LBRP itself).

During the "Qabalistic Cross" beginning and ending of the ritual, you bless yourself in a manner similar to the way a Christian might cross him or herself. However, there are a few key differences. Hover your hand slightly in front of the area being blessed and sense the energy coming through your hand or fingertips touch your body — without actually touching yourself. Also, the cross is formed Up, Down, Right, and Left. Finally, cross your arms in an "X" over your chest, much like an Egyptian mummy. This pose is known in Golden Dawn literature as the Sign of Osiris Risen. In the Qabalistic Cross, the Tree of Life is superimposed over the body and is blessed accordingly.

The Banishing Pentagram of Earth

The Sign of the Enterer

The Sign of Silence (Harpocrates)

The Lesser Banishing Ritual of the Pentagram (Script and Blocking)

Begin the ritual facing east.

I. The Qabalistic Cross

1. Touch your forehead and vibrate "A-Tah"

2. Point towards your feet and "touch" your genitals. Vibrate "Malkuth"

3. Touch your right shoulder and vibrate "Ve-Geburah"

4. Touch your left shoulder and vibrate "Ve-Gedulah"

5. Cross your arms over your chest in the sign of Osiris Risen and vibrate "Le-Olam, Amen."

II. The Pentagrams

1. While facing east, step forward with your left foot and draw the banishing earth pentagram in the air before you. Visualize a pentagram made of bright blue flame. After it is created, step forward with your left foot and extend both of your hands at eye-level into the center of the pentagram (this is known as the "Sign of the Enterer"). Charge it by vibrating the word, "YUD-HEH-VAV-HEH." When the vibration is finished, place your left forefinger to your bottom lip as if you were telling someone to be silent (Sign of Silence/Harpocrates/Hoor-paar-kraat). Extend your right forefinger into the recently charged pentagram and draw a flaming red line as you walk deosil (clockwise) from east to south. Repeat this process for each pentagram, until you are facing east once more and have connected the circular flaming red line.

2. Facing south, draw the pentagram; vibrate the word "AH-DO-NAI."

3. Facing west, draw the pentagram; vibrate the word "EH-HEI-EH."

4. Facing north, draw the pentagram; vibrate the word "AH-GU-LAH."

5. Once again facing east, close the circle and step back into its center. Visualize a pentagram of bright blue flame at each of the four directions, connected by a flaming red line or thread that also surrounds you.

III. The Archangels

1. Take a deep breath and raise and extend your arms up and out to your sides, as if you were being crucified — or about to give someone a really big hug. Visualize four tall, robed, and hooded figures surrounding you, each at a different direction.

2. Say:
Before me RAPHAEL,
Behind me GABRIEL,
To my right hand MICHAEL,
To my left hand URIEL.

For about me flames the pentagram, and in the column inside of me stands the six-rayed star.

Remember to visualize each archangel's robe-color and weapon. When saying, "About me flames the Pentagram," visualize the previously cast pentagrams "flaring" slightly, controlled by your concentration. When you mention the six-rayed star, visualize a bright, golden, yellow hexagram shining from within your heart. It is also advisable to vibrate the name of each archangel.

3. Take a deep breath and, while exhaling through your mouth, let your arms drop slowly to your sides.

Finish the ritual by repeating Step 1, the Qabalistic Cross, and finally close by placing your left forefinger to your bottom lip in the sign of Harpocrates, symbolizing silence. Exhale.

– TETH MYSTERIUM

THE RESTLESS DEAD

*A guide to rescue mediumship,
entity attachment, and spirit release*

AT THE MOMENT of death, there is an inexplicable weight loss of approximately six ounces. Some say that this is the soul's energy moving on to dwell in other dimensions. However, sometimes there may be reasons that a spirit is not ready or able to leave immediately. Then the entity might become earthbound; a shadow-being wandering between this world and the next. Not wanting to part from a loved one, concern that there is unfinished business, or not feeling worthy to go to heaven, are some possible reasons.

Can the spirit of one who has passed away really linger? Can it meddle with the living? A belief in this possibility has been common since prehistoric times. It is hinted at in the spiritual teachings of many cultures around the globe. In the Far East, Feng Shui practitioners offer petitions to appease the hungry ghosts of departed ancestors. In the West, Christian teachings recognize the signs of spirit possession, with exorcism as a possible remedy.

Ed and Lorraine Warren

The 2013 film, *The Conjuring* is based on a true story: a case of entity-attachment, which took place in Connecticut in 1971. Well-known paranormal investigators, Ed and Lorraine Warren were called in to investigate by a family who believed they were troubled by spirits. The Warrens, who emphasized the need for faith in God and prayer when fighting destructive spiritual forces, founded the New England Society for Psychic Research in 1952. They continued lecturing and working in the metaphysical field, until Ed passed away in 2006.

The Warrens first became famous through their involvement in verifying a case of possession in Amityville, New York. This became the basis for a book and another film, *The Amityville Horror.* The plot of both films revolves around expelling harmful spirits that took possession of the living, eventually driving residents from their homes. While the Warrens were very credible, their work did focus on the frightening aspects of afterlife communication. Far from wishing the living harm, most ghostly visitors are friendly and concerned, perhaps intending to be helpful by attaching to the living.

Entity Attachment

The gist of entity attachment is that sometimes conditions arise that permit a departed spirit to enter a living body. Often this follows an accident or other trauma. The victim then appears to change in appearance and personality — to not be the same anymore.

Vulnerability to entity attachment has been reported in the case of donor organ recipients. General health and lifestyle choices may play a role as well. Once attached, entities will usually not leave the host without assistance. The contemporary concept of spirit-release dates to the mid-nineteenth century, when Allan Kardec, the prominent French metaphysical scholar, wrote *The Spirits' Book* (1857) and *The Book of Mediums* (1874).

Entity Release
Another book, Dr. Carl Wickland's *Thirty Years Among The Dead* (1924) popularized the idea of releasing restless and attached spirits. Dr. Edith Fiore's landmark work, *The Unquiet Dead* (1987) furthered the idea that the dead can interfere with and influence the living. Dr. Fiore used case studies of her patients, whom she treated with hypnosis. *Spirit Release Therapy – A Technique Manual* (1992) by William Baldwin offers valuable protocols for releasing both human and non-human entities who have remained a little too close for comfort to the world of the living. *Rescue Mediums*, a twenty-first century cable television program, featured paranormal investigators and mediums from Canada and the UK, who specialized in releasing earthbound spirits, so they could cross freely into the afterlife.

The concept of rescue mediumship is controversial. Some feel that it is wrong to intervene—that a spirit will move forward at the proper time. However, in the case of entity attachment, when a living being becomes a host, taking action to affect a release may be warranted. When an earthbound entity seems to be sad and troubled, rescue mediumship can also be justified.

Simple and Effective Techniques for Entity Release:
Clairvoyants and mediums sometimes report seeing the puzzled and frightened spirits of animals who have been killed on the highway lingering near their bodies. Connecting with the creature's spirit by visualizing pictures of peaceful, safe surroundings, then ringing a bell, will often be sufficient to encourage the soul to move on. Practitioners have been known to travel with a bell handy in their vehicles for this very reason.

In the case of an unwelcome, unwholesome, unhappy entity attached to a human host or to a place, simply lighting a bright yellow candle, then ringing a bell three times, while saying "I release" aloud three times will often be effective. Bright yellow is the color most easily seen in the afterlife and the number three has traditional spiritual implications. Think of past, present, future; the Holy Trinity; body, mind and spirit; and so forth. Finish by scattering salt around the host's residence. This will seal the release and add a layer of protection. Allow the candle to burn out.

– MARINA BYRONY

Moon Cycles

A New Moon rises with the Sun,
Her waxing half at midday shows,
The Full Moon climbs at sunset hour,
And waning half the midnight knows.

NEW	2016	FULL	NEW	2017	FULL
January 9		January 23	January 27		January 12
February 8		February 22	February 26		February 10
March 8		March 23	March 27		March 12
April 7		April 22	April 26		April 11
May 6		May 21	May 25		May 10
June 4		June 20	June 23		June 9
July 4		July 19	July 23		July 9
August 2		August 18	August 21		August 7
September 1, 30*		September 16	September 20		September 6
October 30		October 16	October 19		October 5
November 29		November 14	November 18		November 4
December 29		December 13	December 18		December 3

* Black Moon on September 30

Life takes on added dimension when you match your activities to the waxing and waning of the Moon. Observe the sequence of her phases to learn the wisdom of constant change within complete certainty.

Dates are for Eastern Standard and Daylight Time.

presage

by Dikki-Jo Mullen

ARIES 2015 — PISCES 2016

STRIVING TO UNDERSTAND the unknown and mysterious while finding the courage to move onward and upward amid great changes is the challenge in the coming year. Despite the apparent chaos of the universe, there is order to be found within the wisdom of the stars.

The year to come brings four eclipses in four different zodiac signs: Libra, Virgo, Aries, and Pisces. Breakthroughs can be expected to center around situations ruled by those signs. From the vernal equinox until June 14, 2015 and again September 18 – October 8, 2015 a grand trine forms in the fire signs. Expect to experience great energy, some drama, and a zest for life. Saturn in Sagittarius will square Neptune in Pisces this year, while the Uranus square Pluto aspect which has been in force for the last several years will continue.

Both are long-lasting, unusual, and dynamic planetary patterns promising many shifts in the status quo.

Presage points the way to, in the words of Ralph Waldo Emerson, "make the most of yourself, for that is all there is of you." Begin with your Sun sign, which shines a light on your individual expression and is the focus of your life. Then consider the entry for your Moon sign, which helps in maintaining emotional balance and processing memories. Finally, review the forecast for your ascendant or rising sign. This shows how others see and react to your presence.

The spirituality segments this year are riddles, written for *The Farmer's Almanack* by a brilliant astrologer remembered today only as "Minstrel." The riddles were created between 1820 and 1829, but their wise insights prevail.

ASTROLOGICAL KEYS

Signs of the Zodiac
Channels of Expression

ARIES: fiery, pioneering, competitive
TAURUS: earthy, stable, practical
GEMINI: dual, lively, versatile
CANCER: protective, traditional
LEO: dramatic, flamboyant, warm
VIRGO: conscientious, analytical
LIBRA: refined, fair, sociable
SCORPIO: intense, secretive, ambitious
SAGITTARIUS: friendly, expansive
CAPRICORN: cautious, materialistic
AQUARIUS: inquisitive, unpredictable
PISCES: responsive, dependent, fanciful

Elements

FIRE: Aries, Leo, Sagittarius
EARTH: Taurus, Virgo, Capricorn
AIR: Gemini, Libra, Aquarius
WATER: Cancer, Scorpio, Pisces

Qualities

CARDINAL	FIXED	MUTABLE
Aries	Taurus	Gemini
Cancer	Leo	Virgo
Libra	Scorpio	Sagittarius
Capricorn	Aquarius	Pisces

CARDINAL signs mark the beginning of each new season — active.
FIXED signs represent the season at its height — steadfast.
MUTABLE signs herald a change of season — variable.

Celestial Bodies
Generating Energy of the Cosmos

Sun: birth sign, ego, identity
Moon: emotions, memories, personality
Mercury: communication, intellect, skills
Venus: love, pleasures, the fine arts
Mars: energy, challenges, sports
Jupiter: expansion, religion, happiness
Saturn: responsibility, maturity, realities
Uranus: originality, science, progress
Neptune: dreams, illusions, inspiration
Pluto: rebirth, renewal, resources

Glossary of Aspects

Conjunction: two planets within the same sign or less than 10 degrees apart, favorable or unfavorable according to the nature of the planets.

Sextile: a pleasant, harmonious aspect occurring when two planets are two signs or 60 degrees apart.

Square: a major negative effect resulting when planets are three signs from one another or 90 degrees apart.

Trine: planets four signs or 120 degrees apart, forming a positive and favorable influence.

Quincunx: a mildly negative aspect produced when planets are five signs or 150 degrees apart.

Opposition: a six sign or 180° separation of planets generating positive or negative forces depending on the planets involved.

The Houses — *Twelve Areas of Life*

1st house: appearance, image, identity
2nd house: money, possessions, tools
3rd house: communications, siblings
4th house: family, domesticity, security
5th house: romance, creativity, children
6th house: daily routine, service, health
7th house: marriage, partnerships, union
8th house: passion, death, rebirth, soul
9th house: travel, philosophy, education
10th house: fame, achievement, mastery
11th house: goals, friends, high hopes
12th house: sacrifice, solitude, privacy

Eclipses

Eclipses bring about changes and growth with elements of surprise. For those with a birthday within three days of an eclipse, a year of breakthroughs and important changes can be expected. There will be four eclipses this year: three are total and one is partial.

April 4, 2015   Full Moon Lunar in Libra, north node — total
September 13, 2015   New Moon Solar in Virgo, north node — partial
September 27, 2015   Full Moon Lunar in Aries, south node — total
March 8, 2016   New Moon Solar in Pisces, south node — total

A total eclipse is more influential than a partial and those eclipses conjunct the moon's north node are thought to be most favorable.

Retrograde Planetary Motion

Retrograde motion is an illusion created by Earth's speed relative to the planets. Retrogrades, being quite significant, promise a change of pace and perspective.

Mercury Retrograde

Retrograde Mercury impacts technology, travel, and communication. Those who have been out of touch return. Complete old projects, revise, review, and tread familiar paths. Gemini and Virgo will be affected.

May 19 – June 12, 2015 in Gemini
Sept. 18 – Oct. 10, 2015 in Libra
January 6 – 26, 2016
in Aquarius and Capricorn

Venus Retrograde

Venus retrograde influences art, love, and finances. Taurus and Libra will be affected.

July 26 – September 7, 2015
in Virgo and Leo

Jupiter Retrograde

Large animals, speculation, education, and religion are impacted. Sagittarius and Pisces are affected.

December 9, 2014 – April 9, 2015
in Leo
Jan. 9, 2016 – May 9, 2016 in Virgo

Saturn Retrograde

Elderly people, the disadvantaged, employment, and natural resources are linked to Saturn. Capricorn and Aquarius will be affected.

March 14, 2015 – August 2, 2015
in Sagittarius and Scorpio

Uranus Retrograde

Inventions, science, revolutionaries, and extreme weather relate to Uranus retrograde. Aquarius is impacted.

July 27 – December 26, 2015 in Aries

Neptune Retrograde

Water, aquatic creatures, chemicals, spiritual forces, and psychic phenomena are impacted by Neptune retrograde. Pisces will be affected.

June 13 – November 19, 2015 in Pisces

Pluto Retrograde

Ecology, espionage, birth and death rates, nuclear power, and mysteries relate to Pluto retrograde. Scorpio will be influenced.

April 17 – Sept. 26, 2015 in Capricorn

ARIES

March 20–April 19

Spring 2015 — Spring 2016 for those
born under the sign of the Ram

WITH GREAT natural energy and
dynamism, Aries is the zodiac's competitive, polished and urbane leader.
Impulsive, you are forever at the cross-
roads of the future ready to begin
anew. The emblem for Aries suggests
the horns of the Ram. A straight line
from the forehead divides into two
crescents, showing an outpouring of
extroverted energy.

Spring begins with a flash and a flour-
ish. Mars, your ruler, passes through
Aries until All Fools Day. Wear red,
your favorite color. Welcome the coming season by lighting a ritual fire or
candle garden. April 1 – May 21 your
2nd house is strong, making finances
the focus. You will strive to boost earnings, seeking ways to acquire the possessions you've yearned for. From
late May until the summer solstice the
focus is different. You'll juggle a variety of priorities. Extra travel, negotia-
tions, and the exchange of information
will be a part of this. Be a good listener;
conversations bring valuable clues
which will assure success.

Summer finds benevolent Venus and
Jupiter beginning a long waltz as they
glide together through your 5th house
of love and pleasure. A favorite hobby,
sport, game or artistic project shared
with one you care deeply for make late
June through mid-July an especially
happy cycle. Venus turns retrograde on
July 26, returning to the 5th house by
Lammas Eve where it will remain until
October 8. Express creative ideas and
focus on appreciating beauty and what
gives you pleasure from late summer
until early autumn. A child's accomplishments might add to your joy.

From August 9 through the autumnal equinox Mars moves through Leo,
your fellow fire sign, creating a favorable aspect to your Sun. This influence
generates vitality and enthusiasm. It
will be especially easy for you to take
the initiative and manifest an important
project. The New Moon on August 14
is an excellent time to visualize the specifics. Chant and prepare affirmations.
September accents health; this can
involve the well-being of a loved one.
Consider a variety of wellness options.

The lunar eclipse in Aries on
September 27 brings an abrupt shift in
your usual schedule. Make this a turn
for the better by welcoming new developments. Release the past. Mercury
will impact partnerships of all kinds
throughout September and October.
Others will offer valuable insights by
All Hallows Eve. From November 9
into December, sharing and cooperation
will be essential to success as Venus
and Mars oppose your Sun. Associates
mean well, but they might have a van-
tage point which differs from yours.
At the winter solstice bless relationships. Realize that ties can shift with
the passage of time. Things and people
do change. A legal matter or question

of ethics might be a part of this trend. To honor endings and new beginnings include symbols of Father Time and Baby New Year on your altar.

January 1 – 23 Venus trines your Sun, highlighting your 9th house of spirituality and higher thought. It's a wonderful time to pursue educational interests. Enjoyment of imported items and learning a foreign language can enrich your life. Art, music and poetry offer inspiration, facilitating new faith in the Lord and Lady to sustain you during deep winter. Devote Candlemas observances to career aspirations, as Mercury, Venus and Pluto will cluster near your midheaven. Credibility, reputation, and a desire for promotion are important in mid-February.

Late February through March 20 brings Saturn in Sagittarius into a trine aspect with Uranus, which is transiting your Sun sign of Aries. This is an inventive and progressive cycle. It combines new horizons with the wisdom of precedent and tradition. This alchemy offers valuable foundations for the future. The eclipse on March 8 affects your 12th house. As winter fades into spring, make time for reflection and reverie. It's beneficial to heed dreams and your instincts. Wisdom comes from within. Is there an opportunity to make the world a better place through the pursuit of a charitable project?

HEALTH
The eclipse pattern this year points to profound health changes for either you or a loved one. Be receptive to alternative remedies and new options in approaching wellness. Aries has a special rulership over the head and brain, so good eye care and keeping a positive state of mind are priorities. Late winter promises improved health.

LOVE
Through August 11 benevolent Jupiter is favorably placed in your love sector. A cherished relationship grows toward the level of intimacy you've always longed for. Early June through early October Venus, the celestial love goddess, will move back and forth in a favorable aspect to your Sun, making you particularly charming and charismatic. You'll impress that special someone, with extra attention to good grooming and your wardrobe.

SPIRITUALITY
Like a gentle spring and many a smile, to see and deck Columbia's soil, Tis a spot with freedom crown'd, no more fell winter's howling storm, Augusta's circling plains deform, All the country round. – Minstrel, 1820

This riddle is a reminder that good humor and embracing freedom provide spiritual sustenance.

FINANCE
On August 12 Jupiter enters your 6th house where it will remain through the end of the year. This promises new situations with coworkers and changing your job description. Accept this graciously and profits will accrue. It would be wise to keep a money charm in the workplace; perhaps a coin minted in your birth year, a cowrie shell, or a jade cabochon.

TAURUS
April 20 – May 20

Spring 2015 — Spring 2016 for those
born under the sign of the Bull

LOYALTY, dependability, comfort and
security are the keynotes of Taurus.
Steadfast, you insist upon quality and
the good life. Outwardly you might
appear to be in chaos, but this belies
an inner simplicity, practicality and
reliability. A circle topped with two
inward-facing crescents sketches the
head of the Bull and forms the symbol
for Taurus. It illustrates an all-encom-
passing and solid wholeness, the basis
for outward expression.

A bright note ushers in the spring.
Include music in your meditations and
rituals while celebrating the vernal
equinox. Venus, your ruler, transits your
sign until April 11, attracting both love
and money your way. Creative projects
progress well. It's a good time to visit
an art gallery or to enjoy fine dining.
May Eve – July 8 Mercury makes a
long passage through your 2nd house.
Your thoughts and conversations center
on finances. This time span supports
learning more about your profession.
After Mercury's retrograde ends on
June 12, work-related travel would be
productive. Interview for a new position if you're ready for a change.

The activity accelerates in mid-May;
pressure builds near your birthday. Seek
a constructive outlet. The New Moon
in Taurus on May 18 favors changing
habits for the better and writing a birthday wish list. Secrete it in your Book
of Shadows and review it occasionally
during the year to come.

During June Venus will join Jupiter
in your 4th house, which rules family dynamics and your residence. At
the summer solstice a house blessing
or Feng Shui consultation would
be beneficial. The early summer
favors interior decorating, entertain-
ing at home and real estate transactions. Venus, your ruler, is retrograde
July 26 – September 7. Be patient with
relationships. Resolve to live within
your means. It's best to maintain the
status quo regarding the domestic
situation and personal commitments.
Near Lammastide and again at the
New Moon on August 14 try relaxing
aromatherapy, perhaps lavender or
orange blossom.

In mid-September, as the autumnal
equinox nears, the Sun and Jupiter will
harmonize with your Sun. Life will
become more peaceful. It's favorable
for a vacation. A close relationship
deepens. Enjoy time outdoors with a
loved one. Plan a walk to go bird watch-
ing or photograph beautiful autumn
foliage. Collect some edible wild
plants along the way and add them to
a salad to savor with the elegant picnic
lunch you have packed. September 25 –
November 12 Mars will join Jupiter in
Virgo, sending a high energy, motivat-
ing influence your way. Sports as well
romance and creative projects, such as
clothing design or arts and crafts, bring
exceptional rewards. The Full Moon

in Taurus on October 27 heightens the good times. A memorable ritual followed by a social gathering makes this All Hallows bright with blessings.

The last three weeks of November, a quincunx aspect from two planets in your 6th house accents the fated role animal companions play in your life. Psychic rapport with a cherished familiar deepens. A healing interaction with a highly trained and intelligent service animal can change your life for the better.

December 6 – 30 Venus moves through your relationship sector. Your heart is warmed by the success and happiness of a loved one. Near the winter solstice a message from the spirit world brings peace and comfort, dispelling a regret concerning the past. Legal matters take a turn for the better as the year ends.

Early January – March 5 a Mars opposition ushers in a stimulating and competitive mood. This impacts partnerships of all kinds. Accept others as they are; it's not the time to be overly critical or confrontational. A bit of humor and patience helps to diffuse a tense situation. March 6 – 20 the Sun, Mercury, Venus, and Neptune highlight your 11th house favorably. This is wonderful for networking. Friendships are beneficial; you might become more active within an organization. Community issues, including politics, can be captivating as winter wanes.

HEALTH

The April 4 eclipse in Libra affects your health sector all year. Hereditary traits as well as the everyday environment play a part in wellness. Protect your throat and ears from cold weather. Wear a warm hat and scarf, especially when chilly winds blow. Camphor can be healing. Try rubbing a camphor salve on any problem areas or strewing a few camphor leaves into boiling water, then inhaling the healing steam.

LOVE

Venus will make favorable aspects March 20 – April 11 and October 9 – November 8. Cultivate a relationship with the one who captures your fancy then. January 24 – February 17 a Venus-Pluto conjunction in your 9th house can usher in a soulmate connection with someone who has spent many lives with you. Sharing a past life regression could bring the specifics to light.

SPIRITUALITY

Spreading o'er nature's vast domain, their kisses snatched from Flora's train, while the assenting trees, And slender grass and list'ing lake, for dulcet treasures they partake, Confess the passing breeze. – Minstrel, 1820

This riddle invokes Flora, a goddess of spiritual flowers. Visiting a pastoral scene, among the trees and grasses, perhaps with a sweet breeze blowing over a lake, would deepen your spirituality.

FINANCE

Postpone any risky financial transactions in the spring and early summer when a square from Jupiter and retrograde Venus could tempt you to go out on a financial limb. After September 7 the financial situation improves. January brings prosperity.

GEMINI
May 21 – June 20

Spring 2015 — Spring 2016 for those
born under the sign of the Twins

Diverse, witty Gemini delights at mul-
titasking. While chattering away, you
are adept at getting projects completed.
Unsettled and motivated by great curiosity, your life is truly more about
the journey than the destination. The
Gemini glyph, symbolizing the Twins,
suggests the Roman numeral for two.
The two upright lines are the pillars of
legendary wisdom, while the crossbars
at the top and bottom are cerebral, hinting at intellect.

Spring's first days find Mercury,
your ruler, in your career sector. There
can be confusion as to employment and
career status. If you want to move on,
plan your next move first. April draws
your focus toward love and pleasure. A
new romance or intriguing hobby drives
away the doldrums. A younger person
surprises you with an achievement.
Mid-April through early May Venus
races through your sign. Purchase new
finery or home décor items. Social
situations facilitate financial success.
A great opportunity can come during
a business lunch or conference. Your
charm and popularity are evident.

Mid-May through mid-June Mercury
is retrograde. Be careful to verify
appointments and agreements. Allow

extra time to complete work. Rest. A
sluggish, sleepy quality prevails. By the
New Moon in Gemini on June 16 you'll
be back on track. You'll feel encouraged, empowered and motivated in late
June when Mars completes a conjunction with your Sun. Try a shamanic
emphasis in planning a summer solstice
rite. How about a Native American
sweat lodge or drumming circle?

June 13 – July 8 accents several
favorite activities – travel, writing,
and storytelling — as Mercury moves
rapidly through your sign. The July 4
holiday favors information gathering
and decision making. At the end of
July Venus retrogrades back into your
home and family sector. A misunderstanding among family members is
resolved. Organize, decorate and repair
your dwelling.

At Lammastide a cluster of planets
in your 3rd house sets the pace through
summer's end. You'll be busy, scheduling several short journeys and meetings. A neighbor offers new ideas; a
sibling wants to keep you up to date
with current events. All the while, you
will be in your element, conversing and
exchanging news.

September brings eclipses in your
4th and 11th houses. A change in residence might be in the works soon.
Your thoughts will focus on cherished
long-term goals during the week of
the autumnal equinox. Make a list of
dreams and desires. What do you really
want? Journaling can help with focus
and manifestation.

Throughout October Mercury transits affect your 5th house. Your imagination and creativity will be in top form.

Always a writer at heart, now is the time to pen a romance, biography, or a children's book. Travel for either pleasure, business, or study is favored October 11 – All Hallows Eve. November 9 – December 5 Venus trines your Sun. An avocation could turn into a profitable venture. You'll feel loved and accepted by someone you've wanted to befriend. The excitement builds near the Full Moon in Gemini on November 25. An important question is clarified. The holiday season brings a strong Mars influence; it's a time to be active. Plan a walk to admire the winter scenery. Collect mistletoe or pine cones and add decorative ribbons Surprise loved ones with the seasonal, hand-crafted gifts at the winter solstice.

Restraint is January's watchword. With a mutable T-square aspect and retrograde Mercury, this is not the time to be tempted by risk taking. Thrill-seeking or chances taken with a financial gamble can backfire. Candlemas begins an easier, more relaxed time. Prepare a sabbat altar with lights, corn dollies and affirmations. The New Moon on February 8 accents an upbeat 9th house cycle which uplifts you philosophically through the end of the month. Plan to visit a sacred site, library, or bookstore. In March your career sector is highlighted by several planets, with elusive Neptune prominent. Undercurrents impact professional matters. Subtle signs and cues will steer you in the right direction. Use discretion when it comes to sharing sensitive information, especially near the eclipse on March 8.

HEALTH

The Full Moon on May 3 affects your Scorpio-ruled health sector. Consider health habits. If your diet and lifestyle choices need improvement, make needed adjustments. Since Scorpio is a water sign, the healing qualities of water are helpful. Drink enough liquids, including mineral waters.

LOVE

The eclipse on April 4 explodes in your 5th house of love. Spring ushers in romantic surprises. An existing relationship can move to a new level or there could be a change of heart, signaling that it's time to move on. April 12 – May 7 and November 9 – December 5 are happy regarding love.

SPIRITUALITY

Yonder forest bright and smiling, wears again its native hue beguiling, meadows look with violets a sky and lovely blue.   – Minstrel, 1823

This riddle suggests that changes stimulate spiritual discovery. Beauty and divine power have an ephemeral quality, reflecting the various seasons. The colors shimmer and change as the energy from the sky touches the Earth.

FINANCE

June 25 – August 8 Mars activates your 2nd house of finances. You'll feel the urge to work harder and earn more. This extra effort brings rewards. In mid-August Jupiter enters your 4th house, indicating that the needs of family members or home repairs can impact finances. A real estate bargain can be had before winter is over.

CANCER

June 21 – July 22

Spring 2015 — Spring 2016 for those
born under the sign of the Crab

Reserved, compassionate, and sensitive Cancer intuitively attunes to undercurrents. Natural caregivers, you often form deep attachments to the elderly or the very young. Home and heritage are foremost in your thoughts. The hospitality field or a family business can suit you. The glyph for Cancer suggests the embracing curve of the Crab's claws, holding on with determination while offering shelter.

The vernal equinox welcomes a pleasant 11th house Venus transit. Until April 11, helpful people lend you assistance, offering sincere friendship. The remainder of April through mid-May finds Mars sextile your Sun; the pace quickens. A role model or hero figure inspires you to accept a challenge and be competitive. On May 19 your 12th house of charity is highlighted by Mercury, a trend lasting until July 8. You'll sense the despair of those in need and feel compelled to do some good to offset their difficulties. The welfare and safety of animals can be of concern too. By mid-July Mercury joins Mars and the Sun in your sign. This favors vacation travel, especially near the shore. Collect sea shells to make a treasured keepsake. You'd enjoy visiting historical sites or wandering through antique shops. Do some soul-searching at the New Moon in Cancer on July 15. Identify your priorities and plan your personal journey for the year to come.

Prepare a prosperity ritual blessing to honor Lammas. The Sun, Venus, and Jupiter brighten your 2nd house of finances August 1 – 12, bringing exceptional opportunities to enhance your income. Mid-August through September 17 Saturn completes a long transit through your 5th house. Practical creative expression allows you to release stress. A challenging situation involving a needy child or a dead-end romantic relationship is resolved. This time is wonderful for recycling and for the artistic repurposing of odds and ends. A visit to a thrift shop yields a treasure.

The autumnal equinox accents your home and family sector. Various kinds of memorabilia surface, evoking nostalgia. Assemble a scrapbook or photo album or research your genealogy. The family's past can help you appreciate the present and future. September 27th's eclipse brings prestigious developments regarding your profession. Status concerns you. Secretly, you hope for greater respect and recognition.

Throughout October, Mars affects your 3rd house. This is a dynamic and jittery influence; you're on the go and time passes quickly. It pays to be organized. Before leaving on a journey call ahead to verify appointments and schedules. Transportation can be subject to delay. You would enjoy celebrating All Hallows at home, in quiet reverie surrounded by vintage Halloween decorations.

Early November – January 3 Mars squares your Sun while creating a stir in your home and family sector. Relatives can require extra understanding and support. Seek ways to promote domestic tranquillity and comfort. Make needed household repairs and purchase supplies. At the winter solstice bless your home with a sage smudge. On December 25 the Full Moon in Cancer ushers in elements of the unexpected. This might involve the coming and going of visitors. Meditate on the night sky to find peace and acquire deeper insight.

January 1 – February 13 your 7th house of relationships is affected by several oppositions. Others have ideas to share. Your thoughts will focus on partnership, fairness and balance. Consider all sides of situations before making any decisions. Valentine's Day – March 5 Mars favors your pleasure and love sector. Someone special to you is attentive and caring. Quality time together involves sports, hobbies, or games. The eclipse on March 8, tinged by Neptune, foreshadows a change in your beliefs and spiritual preferences during the last weeks of winter. Investigate the claims of gurus, spiritual healers, and teachers carefully. They might not be as they seem. Watch omens, observe synchronicities and interpret dreams. Your guardian angel or spirit guide is sending an important message.

HEALTH

Saturn, always important to health, transits your 6th house of health from the vernal equinox until June 14. It returns on September 18 to remain in that position for more than two years. Address any potential health needs during the spring and summer. Consider scheduling an overall checkup near your birthday to make sure all is well. In the autumn focus on maintaining good health habits.

LOVE

Pluto, ruler of your love sector, will be retrograde April 17 – September 26. Healing from old heartaches or the return of a long-lost love is likely then. Offer a bouquet of summer herbs and flowers to your favorite lunar deity at the Full Moon on July 1 while affirming a blessing upon your soul mate relationship.

SPIRITUALITY

O! thou prime of the year, delightful bright appear, Oft votive at thy shrine; for soon thou wilt bow to time's hand, With the amber wand, rosy hours reign.
– Minstrel, 1820

This riddle is a reminder about the length of days at midsummer, marking time, the most precious of assets. Amber is a gem once thought to be tears dropped by the Sun. The amber wand honors the solar power. The rosy hours herald the sunset and nod to the Moon, Cancer's ruler.

FINANCE

From the vernal equinox until August 11 lucky Jupiter will transit your 2nd house of finances. Make the most of opportunities to add to your income which arise then, and you will establish a pattern which assures lasting security.

167

LEO

July 23–August 22

Spring 2015 — Spring 2016 for those
born under the sign of the Lion

Warm, dramatic Leo has an innate flair for guiding others. Dignified and good humored, you gracefully combine business with pleasure. The glyph for Leo suggests the curve of the Lion's tail reaching from the ground, circling toward the Sun, then swirling back, bringing energy toward the Earth.

Springtime welcomes you with a burst of enthusiasm and a sense of purpose. In March five placements in fire signs form a grand trine. You'll excel in the arts, academics, or projects involving leadership. The lunar eclipse on April 4 affects your 3rd house. A neighbor or family member voices interesting insights which enhance your awareness. Make choices concerning travel and transportation during April.

May emphasizes your 11th house. Friends enlist your assistance regarding an organization, perhaps inviting you to join an advisory board. This brings unexpected opportunities to do good deeds. June 1 – 24 a Mars sextile brings adjustments involving the roles associates play in your life. Friends offer fresh perspectives. Venus affects your 1st house in June, adding to your charm and charisma. Celebrate the summer solstice adorned in beautiful flowers

and jewels. Invoke the goddess' blessings regarding heartfelt passions.

In early July your 12th house is influenced by Mars and the Sun. This focus is introspective. You'll seek time for meditation and reflection. The New Moon in Cancer on July 15 stimulates your flair for healing and problem solving. July 24 – August 7 Mercury races through Leo. You'll communicate with exceptional eloquence. This is a marvelous time for teaching, writing and travel. Lammastide may find you journeying to a conference or gathering.

At the New Moon in Leo on August 14, Mercury and Jupiter highlight your 2nd house of possessions and income. Consider the significance of money and valuables. It's a good time to shop for an important item you've yearned for. Select a special something to brighten your birthday.

September finds Mars in the midst of Leo, a trend which lasts through the autumnal equinox. This fiery, energetic influence can make you prone to extremes. Control anger and impatience. Exercise can help. Aim toward constructive outcomes when making choices and all will be well. On September 18 Saturn begins a favorable aspect to your Sun which lasts through the winter. A responsibility becomes a labor of love. Your imaginative ideas generate rewards near the time of the September 27 eclipse.

October finds practical matters prevailing. Earth sign transits highlight your 2nd and 6th houses, bringing a productive schedule regarding employment. If a pay raise is desired, seek ways to increase efficiency. Time spent outdoors, perhaps accompanied by an animal companion, would be worthwhile. At All Hallows honor the change in seasons by adding gourds and dried grasses to the altar. During the first three weeks of November the Sun and Mercury highlight domestic matters. Loved ones communicate plans and concerns. Just by listening, a simple misunderstanding can be rectified.

December finds a Venus influence brightening your home sector. Fun and friendship center around your home. A family member has news of success to share. January 1 – 23 brings favorable transits in your sector of love and pleasure. Pursue a favorite avocation. A loved one would appreciate an outing to the theater, a concert or art gallery. The Full Moon in Leo on January 23 reveals how you impact others. Draw down the Moon with the intent of developing your higher self.

Candlemas finds Mercury, Venus and Pluto in your health sector. Affirm wellness at the sabbat. Light seven candles, one in each of the chakra colors, to shed light upon your body's needs. The last half of February finds your 7th house setting the pace. Partnerships, business as well as personal, are especially important. Others make plans for you and voice their expectations.

Late winter is influenced by the March 8 eclipse in your 8th house. The afterlife, messages from loved ones who have passed away, and friendly ghosts are prevalent. Hidden truths come to light, a puzzle is solved and research projects are fruitful — all by March 19.

HEALTH

The planet of age-appropriate considerations and habits, Saturn, rules your health sector. Be aware of how your body changes over time. Patience is essential in reaching fitness goals. The early winter brings improved vitality.

LOVE

June 6 – October 8 Venus makes a very long transit through Leo. The celestial love goddess, supported by Uranus and Saturn, brings exceptional happiness during this time. There is potential to build a wonderful relationship. Wear coral and bright green, colors linked to Venus, to heighten the bliss.

SPIRITUALITY

Lake's cool recess now we find, a beauteous calm retreat. Our parching thirst we here unbind; By shade secured from heat. – Minstrel, 1827

This riddle reveals how seeking calmness and a quiet environment will refresh the soul. Cherish coolness; enjoy a sip of water to offset stress and excessive brightness.

FINANCE

From the vernal equinox until August 11 Jupiter conjoins your Sun, bringing genuine abundance. The spring and summer sparkle with financial opportunities. Pursue them in order to add to your security for a long time to come. The eclipse on September 13 affects your money sector. Adapt to new financial priorities and changes in your source of income then and all will be well throughout the rest of the year.

VIRGO

August 23 – September 22

Spring 2015 — Spring 2016 for those
born under the sign of the Virgin

Doing everything the right way is the essence of this precise and particular birth sign. Often personal priorities are set aside to heal and encourage those who are in need. Three straight vertical lines connected at the top with a curved line turned up and out forms Virgo's glyph. This illustrates three layers of consciousness connected to a super conscious awareness with an introverted, earthy ultimate focus.

From the vernal equinox through All Fools Day people challenge your patience and good humor. Mercury, your ruler, will oppose your Sun and square Saturn. Some teaching and explaining would be helpful. During April several transits, including Venus, in your 9th house emphasize spirituality, learning, and foreign travel. Your flair for languages helps you to communicate easily with those from other lands. May Eve accents career paths. At the sabbat cherish and visualize your professional ambitions. Status, competition and credibility will remain important throughout May.

June begins on a hectic note. Retrograde Mercury is in a T-square aspect pattern with several mutable sign planets. After June 12 matters calm down and it's easier to make progress both at home and work. Humanitarian interests highlight the week of the summer solstice. Dedicate the sabbat rites to blessing those in need. This can extend to animals and ecological issues.

July favors networking and promotional work as water sign planets are in your 11th house. It's a great time to make connections. Forge deeper bonds of friendship near the New Moon on July 15. July 19 – 31 Venus lightly kisses your 1st house. A sweet and courtly interlude with a romantic prospect brings a hint of greater happiness to come. Purchase some new finery or flowers for the Lammastide celebration. Select sunshine hues of gold, peach and crimson.

In mid-August Jupiter, the most fortunate of planets, enters Virgo for a year-long stay. Your world widens; great opportunities are about to materialize. Expand your dreams and pursue your heart's desire. Your birthday augurs changes and surprises this year. There is an eclipse in your sign on September 13. The past dissolves. Make a place in your life for a new situation. It could be time for a job change or residential move.

The autumnal equinox finds plans and priorities in flux, as Mercury will be retrograde. A traditional sabbat celebration, followed by simple platters of seasonal fruit and vegetables with fresh bread would be good. Dreams hearkening back to your childhood or past lives drift through your thoughts in late September through early October.

October 9 – November 8 Venus joins Jupiter in Virgo to usher in a really upbeat cycle. Creativity, cultural interests and, above all, romantic love are favored. Plan to celebrate All Hallows strengthening your relationship. Your heart is healed of grief because transcendent messages of comfort come from the spirit world. The remainder of November accents your 2nd house of finances. Balance accounts; analyze expenses and earnings. Plan shopping excursions in preparation for the winter holiday season.

December concerns living arrangements and household maintenance. Bless and give thanks for your home and family at the New Moon on December 11. From the winter solstice through January 1 and again January 9 – 20 the Sun and Mercury brighten your 5th house of pleasure and love. Holiday travel is favored. Outdoor recreation, beautiful winter scenery, or spiritual programs would be enjoyable.

Late January – February 17 Venus joins Pluto and forms a wonderful aspect to your Sun. A true love connection deepens. Plan your leisure hours and vacation time. Artistically inclined Virgos will experience creative breakthroughs.

The February 22 Full Moon in Virgo opposes Neptune. Peer pressure is pronounced. Illusion is afoot. How are the opinions of others affecting your choices?

March 1 – 12 a strong 6th house transit emphasizes your favorite subject, health. Select nutritious foods and a fitness program. Friends offer new health and medical news. Winter's last days bring planetary transits to your relationship sector. Teamwork and supportive commitments will be important.

HEALTH

Address any counterproductive health habits July 27 – December 26 when Uranus, ruler of your 6th house of health, is retrograde. Your past holds the key to future wellness. Weather and temperature will impact how well you feel all year. Dress comfortably to cope with climatic extremes.

LOVE

September 25 – November 12 passionate Mars transits earthy Virgo. A relationship deepens and moves forward. Your feelings are reciprocated. How about planning a camping trip, planting a garden together, or strolling through a beautiful park?

SPIRITUALITY

On nature's face there's many a smile, Which luxury and peace betoken; it pays the laborer for his toil, His health, his joy, his rest unbroken.

— Minstrel, 1829

This riddle is a reminder of Mother Nature's consciousness. She rewards diligence with the rich harvest of wholesome peace and spiritual nourishment.

FINANCE

April 4 and September 27 bring eclipses in your 2nd and 8th houses of finance. Elements of the unexpected promise changes in your source of income or financial strategies. Unplanned expenses might arise. When lucky Jupiter enters your sign in mid-August, the long-term financial picture begins to brighten. By year's end the money situation is good.

LIBRA
September 23 – October 23
Spring 2015 — Spring 2016 for those
born under the sign of the Scales

A life balanced by significant relationships is a priority, as Libra finds fulfillment through companionship. Your
love of harmony guides you to develop
exceptional people skills. Libra's glyph
shows a straight lower line symbolizing the physical world and an upper
line with a crescent. This suggests the
Sun on the horizon, showing the equal
balance between day and night at the
autumnal equinox.

Your life is about to change dramati-
cally. There is a total lunar eclipse in
Libra on April 4; Mars, Mercury, and
the Sun are in opposition to you. Others
are talkative and independent. Listen
and work out a compromise. Venus,
your ruler, moves through Gemini and
restores harmony April 12 – May 7.
Your 9th house is highlighted, reminding you to have faith and to learn from
recent experiences. Mid-May through
the summer solstice Mars trines your
Sun, bringing renewed physical vitality. Plans to travel or undertake new
studies motivate you; the New Moon
on June 16 reveals specifics. At the
summer solstice begin a journal or add
to your Book of Shadows. Simply writing down goals and wishes often results
in their manifestation.

Early June – July 18 Venus is in Leo,
in mutual reception with your Sun.
Gracious, almost magical options materialize, allowing you to get out of any
difficult situations. Creativity helps you
meet professional goals. Talented, helpful people lend assistance. Just before
Lammastide Venus turns retrograde
until September 7. Budget carefully;
it's tempting to overextend finan-
cially. Preserve the status quo in both
business and personal partnerships. A
light, friendly attitude helps you cope
with ill-mannered individuals. There
might be some bad behavior to tolerate in others between Lammastide
and Labor Day.

As September opens, Mercury begins
a long passage through your sign, lasting until November 2. It's a great time
to write for publication or undertake
new studies. The September 13 eclipse
in your 12th house brings an unchar-
acteristic need to be alone. Forgiving
a character flaw or accepting a disap-
pointment can be a part of this. The
September 27 eclipse affects your 7th
house of relationships. A close partnership could move in a different direction.
Hesitate if considering involvement in
legal matters. There might be a hidden
caveat making it not worth the expense
or trouble.

In October a strong emphasis on cardinal signs keeps you busy with home,
business, and relationship situations.
Once Mercury goes direct on October
10 it's easy to move forward. Much is
accomplished following the New Moon
in Libra on October 12 if you take time
to affirm what you most desire for the
year ahead. Realization of goals is

always accomplished through early planning and an equal amount of attention to the details.

November 9 – December 5 Venus in Libra brightens your 1st house. Public speaking in any form holds the potential for great success now. By remaining true to yourself, you'll find doors of opportunity opening. The holiday season brings a challenging, competitive mood. Mars conjoins your Sun and squares Pluto through December to January 3. Don't go to extremes regarding sports or other strenuous activities. Consider the consequences before acting, especially near the Full Moon on December 25. At the same time December finds you motivated and more decisive than usual.

In January Venus joins Saturn in Sagittarius, activating your 3rd house. A sibling or neighbor appreciates your assistance. Consider updating your phone or computer. Staying in touch and being aware of news can be especially vital. Honor Candlemas at home as a cluster of planets, including Pluto, affect your sector of home and family in early February.

Late February through mid-March your sector of love and pleasure enjoys a prominent influence from transits in the sign of Aquarius. You will be aware of how cherished you are by a loved one. Winter's final days bring intuitive interchanges with beloved animal companions with Mercury, the Sun and Neptune gathered in your 6th house. You will be aware of how healing the love and devotion of an animal really is.

HEALTH

The total eclipse on March 8, 2016, profoundly affects your health. Attune to your body's needs, including regular medical checkups. The health of your whole body will benefit from a foot massage, pedicure, or reflexology.

LOVE

The Venus retrograde of July 26 – September 7 can bring some challenges in love regarding mutual friends or membership in organizations that are important to you. Be a good, supportive friend during this time and, for now don't change your relationship status. September's eclipse pattern reveals how those closest to you are growing and changing.

SPIRITUALITY

Lovely autumn how delicious are thy varied bounties, And thy rip'ning clusters precious, Gently soothing away each and every care. – Minstrel, 1823

The riddle blesses the autumn time of life, when precious fruits ripen following labor and effort. Time is the greatest healer of disappointments and reliever of worries.

FINANCE

June 15 – September 17 Saturn completes a challenging transit through your financial sector which began back in October 2012. And at this time a financial obligation can be resolved. Autumn and winter will favor gain. Since Scorpio rules your financial sector, past life karma and inherited or invested money often factor in to your cash flow.

SCORPIO
October 24 – November 21
Spring 2015 — Spring 2016 for those
born under the sign of the Scorpion

The complex Scorpion delves beneath the surface of things, anxious to illuminate hidden truths. You are all about intensity, while often appearing lighthearted on the surface. Scorpio's glyph is formed by three lines representing the Scorpion's tail. The fore stroke suggests research and preparation. The lines are the higher, lower, and evolving states of mental consciousness. The final barb represents the struggle to rise above base temptation.

Spring begins with a Mercury-Neptune emphasis. Your words and thoughts involve expressing creative ideas and planning vacations. Children can delight you near the vernal equinox. April finds planetary transits in Taurus, your opposing sign. Others stubbornly express different ideas and preferences. Arguments end in moot points; so relax, smile and adopt a "live and let live" attitude. Pluto, your ruler, is retrograde April 17 – September 26. Wise guidance comes through recalling memories of past experiences. Studies undertaken or skills previously developed have new uses applicable to your present and future.

Weave a protective garland of flowers on May Eve to wear through the Scorpio Full Moon on May 3. This lunation ushers in a four-week span during which you'll have a heightened zest for life. You'll gain experience and knowledge. May 8 – June 5 Venus glides through your 9th house. Exotic foods and beverages are appealing. Visit an import shop or dine out in a restaurant featuring foreign cuisine. During mid to late June planets in your 8th house bring contact with the spirit world. Other dimensions of reality are in evidence. Near the summer solstice take a ghost tour, attend a séance, or stroll through a historic graveyard. You'll experience genuine wonderment and awe.

During July and early August Mars marches through Cancer, drumming in an upbeat, energizing rhythm. Much is accomplished almost effortlessly. Enjoy water sports during summer's warm, bright days. At Lammastide walk outdoors early in the morning. A garden plant offers a message to you regarding the spirit of the early harvest. August 8 – 27 Mercury races through your 11th house. Friends voice suggestions. Your social circle widens. Plans for the future occupy your thoughts during September. At the autumnal equinox prepare a healing talisman or brew herbal tonics for wellness. The lunar eclipse on September 27 impacts your health sector. Maintain a positive state of mind to enhance physical well-being.

October 1 – 8 Venus completes a passage over your midheaven. Your charm and talent have impressed associates. Accolades and recognition are likely. Socialize with coworkers.

October 9 – 26 strong 12th house indicators deepen your concern for those in need. You might want to volunteer with a charity. The Full Moon on October 27 brightens All Hallows activities. A partner or coven member suggests participation in a group ritual. This becomes a powerful spiritual experience.

November finds your 1st house strong, emphasizing your vibrant personality. Mercury races past your Sun November 3 – 20, generating a flurry of messages and travel opportunities. The New Moon in Scorpio on November 11 freshens your outlook. The winter holiday season promises much joy and gain. Benevolent Venus shines in your sign December 6 – 30. At the winter solstice delectable holiday foods tempt you. Old St. Nick leaves a gift you've wanted under the Christmas tree. Life is good on New Year's Eve, with much to be grateful for.

Early January through early March accents fiery Mars. Take constructive action to ease frustration and impatience. Retrograde Mercury January 6 – 26 indicates a temporary change of mind. Don't burn bridges; keep your options open. Candlemas brings stability. Select yellow tapers for mental clarity and a golden topaz, your birth stone, for inspiration as you celebrate the sabbat. An amusing visitor arrives near the New Moon on February 8. During February celestial influences in your 4th house favor real estate transactions, home repairs, or decorating. March brings a surprise regarding romance. The total eclipse on March 3 is of the heart, right in the middle of your love sector. Happily, Venus makes a favor-

able sign change on March 13, bringing the blessing of true love as winter ends.

HEALTH

June 15 – September 17 a Saturn-Sun aspect helps you define health goals. It's a time when plenty of rest is essential. Since water signs are involved, time spent near the shore can be therapeutic. Include sea salt or seafood in your diet.

LOVE

Venus impacts your 10th house of career from early June until early October. A romantic relationship can develop with a professional associate or through an introduction made by a coworker. Your skill at and enjoyment of your career field favorably impresses a special someone.

SPIRITUALITY

Old Orchard's flavor now inspires the rustic laborer's song; and now in transports he admires His heavy fields of corn. – Minstrel, 1827

The riddle glorifies the end of the harvest, a metaphor for death and rebirth. Fulfillment comes following the end of important work.

FINANCE

Jupiter, ruler of your financial sector, forms a favorable sextile aspect from August 12 through the end of winter. Opportunities for monetary gain arise. Follow through with what the universe presents. Do your part, and you will prosper.

SAGITTARIUS
November 22 – December 21
Spring 2015 — Spring 2016 for those
born under the sign of the Archer

Holding a bow and arrow forever pointed toward wider horizons, Sagittarius is on a perpetual quest of discovery. You are idealistic and seek to understand life's highest potentials. The glyph for Sagittarius is the arrow of the Archer, with a dividing crossbar hinting at duality, indecision and restlessness. The lower part of the shaft suggests an animal nature, while the tip points to expression of great physical and intellectual energy.

Early spring favors quiet reflection. Jupiter, your ruler, is retrograde until April 9. This might involve a spiritual retreat, as your 9th house is highlighted. Finish any partially completed projects. Mid-April through May 7 a Venus transit through your sector of partnership has you rejoicing at the success of someone close to you. Dedicate May Eve rites to blessing your closest relationships. By mid-May Mars will oppose your Sun. This competitive influence lasts until June 24. Don't make demands or issue ultimatums. Remain good-humored. Approach volatile situations like a game and all will be well. The Full Moon in Sagittarius on June 2 pivots around several mutable sign placements and ushers in a very

busy cycle. Get organized to relieve stress and move forward during the weeks before the summer solstice.

July brings a sense of reprieve as Saturn will have exited your birth sign. This lighter, more relaxed tone lingers until September 18, when Saturn reenters Sagittarius. July 24 – August 7 favors study, travel and public speaking as a grand trine in fire signs is emphasized by Mercury. From mid-August through the autumnal equinox, Venus and Mars trine your Sun bringing enhanced vitality and charisma. Enjoyment of various creative projects, social gatherings and sports will peak during late summer.

October brings Venus, Mars and Jupiter together in Virgo, your 10th house of fame and fortune. Opportunities for professional recognition are present. Greater respect and status are likely. Remain dedicated and make an extra effort. Unexpected developments can take your ambitions in a new direction. Talkative friends offer ideas concerning the All Hallows celebration, as Mercury affects your 11th house.

November 1 – 12 brings a contemplative mood, as your 12th house is accented. Avoid crowds, enjoy a solitary walk, revel in the late autumn scenery and heed nature's omens. On November 13 Mars changes signs and will sextile your Sun, an aspect which remains until early January. This is a very social influence, and invitations to various gatherings arrive. Mercury conjoins your Sun November 21 – December 9. You will be exceptionally eloquent, and your words can inspire others. Write a yuletide poem or story and make copies to include with holiday gifts and cards. Travel appeals to you near your birthday. From the winter solstice through December 31 your 2nd and 8th houses of finances, earnings and investments are activated. The Full Moon in Cancer on December 25 illuminates the specifics. Devote spiritual rites to prosperity magic. Budgeting, freecycling and bargain hunting are worthwhile now.

Venus enters your sign as the New Year begins. January 1 – 23 adds beauty to your life through love, music and creative projects. Jupiter turns retrograde in your career sector by mid-January, a trend which continues through the end of winter. Be aware of repeating patterns at work. Manage your time wisely. Your reputation precedes you. At Candlemas reflect upon healing troubled memories. Light candles with the intent of understanding and releasing the past while brightening a clear path toward the future. February 8 – 29 brings Aquarius transits to your 3rd house. Inspirational ideas arise during conversations. The time passes quickly, and you'll be busy.

Mars enters Sagittarius on March 6. Your energy level will be exceptional the rest of the month. Home life and living arrangements are changing due to the total solar eclipse on March 8. A move is possible. Your mood is fiery. Control impatience and anger as winter ends.

HEALTH
Venus, ruler of your 6th house of health, is retrograde July 26 – September 7. It's a good time to analyze patterns and correct counterproductive health habits. Always keep consumption of tempting sweets and alcohol at a minimum to control blood sugar. Select foods which are good for your liver.

LOVE
The eclipse on September 27 falls in your 5th house of love, bringing a whirlwind of romantic activity during autumn and winter. An established relationship might end or enter a new phase. An intriguing, new romantic encounter promises elements of surprise.

SPIRITUALITY
The rider blasts along the plain, Now come to us remind, To look for winter's rougher train, In storms of angry wind.
                                    – Minstrel, 1827

The riddle's message is to ride enthusiastically forward to meet life, regardless of how challenging situations might seem. Seeking life's storms while confronting adversaries is the path which eventually leads to a broader spiritual perspective.

FINANCE
Be conservative regarding financial decisions in July when oppositions to your money sector can lead to impulsive spending. Consider major purchases carefully and seek the best prices. Don't leave your job during the summer without planning ahead. The New Moon on January 9, 2016, favorably affects your 2nd house of earned income, beginning a good four-week cycle for seeking either a pay raise or extra work to generate more income.

CAPRICORN
December 22 – January 19

Spring 2015 — Spring 2016 for those
born under the sign of the Goat

Direct and dignified, the Goat strives to establish respect and security. You approach your desired goal by steadily advancing step by step, eventually arriving at the summit of success. Capricorn's glyph forms a stylized curve outlining the Goat's head. A line of intellect moves straight down to the plane of earthly matter then rises heavenward to end in a crescent, twisting into a final circle of spirit.

Devote the vernal equinox sabbat to love affirmations. Invoke your favorite goddess of romance. Venus brightens your 5th house of affection and pleasure through mid-April. On April 4 an eclipse creates a stir in your 10th house of career success and professional accomplishments. Prepare for an upset in the balance of power around you. This will ultimately work in your favor. April 18 – 30 Mercury is supportive. Express creativity, enjoy sports, travel for pleasure, or invite someone you love along on a sightseeing journey.

During May and June several Gemini transits, including Mars, impact your health sector. Seek ways to relieve stress and to keep your daily environment safe and comfortable. Moderate exercise is good. Your past health history contains valuable clues concerning wellness while Mercury is retrograde May 19 – June 12. The New Moon on June 16 marks a turn for the better regarding your health. From mid-June through the summer solstice, 8th house Venus and Jupiter transits indicate that a spouse's or partner's earning potential will improve significantly. Your tax return, an insurance settlement, or investment income can add to your personal coffers.

The Capricorn Full Moon on July 1 emphasizes high standards of excellence. You are inspired and will shine like a star. Mars transits your opposing sign of Cancer throughout July until August 8. Dynamic, competitive acquaintances encourage you to grow. Dedicate Lammastide observances to restoring harmony. Prepare and bless a peace symbol to wear or display. In mid-August your 9th house is strong. Your spiritual strength is heightened; your faith consoles you. Devote extra time to studies or a writing project. Follow current events. The final weeks of summer bring workable solutions, helping you to rise above difficulties.

Shortly after the autumnal equinox Pluto finishes its retrograde cycle in your sign. A sense of rebirth prevails as September ends. October emphasizes your 10th house of career and achievement. Projects require your immediate attention. Business meetings and communication are important. The New Moon in Libra on October 12 exactly opposes Uranus in Aries. Startling choices between family situations and career aspirations come to the fore. At All Hallows you'll perceive the spiritual nuances in nature, including wildlife. Decorate the altar with potted herbs and colored leaves. Consider a faux fur animal costume.

By mid-November Mars will cross your midheaven, setting an energetic tone for the holiday season. You'll be highly visible. A position of leadership might be offered to you near the winter solstice. Quick and clever Mercury enters your sign December 10 – January 1 and retrogrades back in again January 9 – February 13. Your intellectual energy will be high, and you'll easily make wise choices. An invitation to travel brightens your birthday. Research your destination thoroughly and plan your itinerary before departure.

Expect a truly upbeat cycle for love and money when Venus transits Capricorn January 24 – February 17. Place rose red tapers on the Candlemas altar with heart and cupid decorations. Late February finds Mars in your 11th house to focus upon the future. Friends include you in projects involving politics or other community activities.

In March several transits join Neptune in your 3rd house. Keep a clear state of mind; support imaginative hunches with facts. Daydreams and visions are prevalent near the time of the eclipse on March 8. A kindly spirit or guardian angel hovers nearby. Other planes of existence and dimensions of reality are quite tangible during the last days of winter.

HEALTH

Saturn, which always impacts health and the aging process, begins a long passage through your 12th house this year. This shows that taking quiet time for reverie and meditation and getting adequate sleep will add to your well-being. Trust your intuition when making decisions concerning health care.

LOVE

Venus, ruler of your 5th house of love, favors romance very early in the springtime and again during the winter months, particularly near Candlemas. The New Moon in Taurus on May 18 ushers in an excellent four-week cycle for nurturing a more intimate, loving relationship with one whom you cherish.

SPIRITUALITY

Soon shall winter's sullen storms, these lovely images deform, with iron grasp shake every bough, lay the greenery honors low, nor let the streams ever move. – Minstrel, 1820

This riddle is a reminder that, like the winter, the spiritual journey of humanity is marked by storms. Seasons of experience sweep away the past, just as last year's greens and flowers inevitably fade away.

FINANCE

A benevolent, year-long Jupiter aspect begins in mid-August, bringing a streak of promising financial prospects. However, the eclipse on September 27 affects your sector of property and housing. Expenses related to household upkeep or a real estate transaction can be costly in the autumn and winter months. Place a Feng Shui cure for prosperity in your home.

AQUARIUS
January 20–February 18
Spring 2015 — Spring 2016 for those born under the sign of the Water Bearer

Sharing is the mission, hints the Water Bearer, while bringing refreshment to all of humanity. Original and complex, you treasure freedom yet your social circle is a priority. The glyph for Aquarius shows two waves of angular lines which never touch, suggesting detachment and intellect. It illustrates the magnetism and flow of pure, pulsing, electrical current freely dispersed from the Water Bearer's jar.

The early spring finds Jupiter retrograde in your 7th house. You are busy offering counsel and encouragement to an overly optimistic partner or spouse who has become disheartened. The April 4 eclipse in Libra brings fascination with faraway places. Travel and imported items can be on your wish list. You will be captivated by different spiritual traditions and might explore an unfamiliar religion during April.

On May Eve Mercury enters your 5th house of love and pleasure where it will remain until July 8. You will enjoy conversing with an attractive person. There is a romantic sparkle developing. May 13 – June 24 a passionate Mars influence fans the flame of desire. By the summer solstice a significant relationship solidifies. Sit in the bright sunlight on the longest of days to write affirmations concerning your deepest emotional needs and thoughts about the future. The pages might become a love letter or poem.

July finds the Sun and Venus affecting your 7th and 8th houses. Others present financial plans and suggestions. This elicits a mixed reaction from you. Make a special effort to respect and understand opposing viewpoints. Under the light of the Full (Blue) Moon in Aquarius on July 31, meditate on whether to pursue a serendipitous opportunity. At Lammastide, the next day, consult the Tarot or tea leaves for added insight about making the right decision. Throughout August until September 17 Saturn will dominate your midheaven, making a strong square aspect to your Sun. Career pathways are accented; consider your professional goals and ambitions. Conscientious effort on your part will enhance your credibility and secure your status.

The eclipse on September 13 in your sector of mysteries can make you aware of the afterlife in a new way. A spirit visitation or past life recollection can be a part of this. At the autumnal equinox an in-law, grandparent or grandchild expresses love and concern. The September 27 eclipse affects transportation and communication. The purchase of a new vehicle or computer can be considered as the month ends. Devote October to truth seeking and research. Virgo transits will highlight your 8th house, encouraging you to delve beneath the surface of events. All Hallows brings awareness of the afterlife. Create an ancestor altar. Assemble vintage garments to create a comfortable, one-of-a-kind costume.

November 9 – December 5 a Venus aspect favors holiday decorating, cooking, and shopping. During the last three weeks of December Sagittarius transits, including Saturn, will activate your 11th house. Charitable projects and community service bring new types of people into your life. Celebrate the winter solstice by placing a globe upon your altar. Encircle it with pictures or statues of people from various countries. Dedicate the sabbat to diversity and world peace.

January finds your 12th house affected by Capricorn transits, including Pluto. Tired of crowds, you'll yearn to spend time alone or with your nearest and dearest. The warm company of a beloved, affectionate animal promises happiness during the coldest weeks of the year.

At Candlemas place a blue candle near a window to guide wayfarers to their destinations or to welcome an absent loved one safely home. Your birthday finds you considering how to improve your personal appearance. The New Moon in Aquarius on February 8 ushers in a strong 1st house influence. You will examine your preferences and skills, seeking deeper self awareness.

In early March recognize financial parameters. Define exactly where you are regarding security and income. The eclipse on March 8 brings an urge to be free of material concerns. You might abandon a dead-end job. Your attitude about finances will be in flux during the last weeks of winter.

HEALTH

Changes in temperature, wind, air pressure, and humidity affect your vitality. Make your environment physically comfortable during extreme weather patterns. The Moon rules your health sector. Observe how you feel during the lunar phases and daily Moon sign changes in order to best attune to your health cycles.

LOVE

Springtime brings a flurry of activity in your love sector. A romantic connection which develops from April through June can deepen into a lasting bond this year. Invite a loved one to travel to a romantic destination such as Paris, Hawaii, or Miami Beach when the Full Moon falls in your 5th house during the week of November 25.

SPIRITUALITY

The blasts of winter rage around, and fires the driving storm; A snowy mantle for the ground to nourish and to warm.
                                    – Minstrel, 1827

The riddle describes a fierce desolation which freezes the Water Bearer's life-giving liquid. The spiritual message is one of adaptability and maintaining faith that all is well despite temporary blockages.

FINANCE

Be realistic about finances this year. The eclipses on September 13 and March 8 indicate shifts in your sources of income or expenses. Gather details, plan ahead, and consider options regarding your money from March 21 – 31, then the year will be profitable.

PISCES

February 19 – March 20

Spring 2015 — Spring 2016 for those
born under the sign of the Fish

The gentle, empathetic Fish plays the
roles of best buddy and problem solver
to many different acquaintances. It's
important to maintain boundaries to
avoid drifting into situations that are not
quite what was anticipated. The Pisces
glyph shows a horizontal line, representing matter, linking two back-to-
back crescents. This suggests two fish,
linked yet swimming apart, torn by
perpetual conflicts between the head
and heart.

A prominent Mercury transit emphasizes mobility from the vernal equinox
until March 31. Explore ideas; curiosity
motivates you. Mars impacts your 3rd
house during April. Concentrate on your
schedule. A neighbor reaches out, making a request and offering friendship.
April 13 – May 7 Venus brightens your
sector of home and family.

Mid-May through late June brings
volatile influences involving mutable
signs. Usually you avoid conflict, but
now it's preferable to face clashes
directly. Matters improve near the New
Moon on June 16. By the summer solstice bygones will be bygones. Offer a
ritual blessing requesting forgiveness
and cooperation.

During July Mercury and the Sun
will play tag with Mars in Cancer,
your sister water sign. This ushers in
a delightful time accenting waterfront
recreation and creative expression.
Peace and emotional fulfillment prevail. Devote Lammastide to offering
thanks for the abundance of goodness
and beauty in your life.

August 1 – October 8 Venus transits your 6th house, promising good
health, enjoyable working conditions,
and camaraderie among coworkers.
You bask in the admiration of others
near the Full Moon in Pisces on August
29. Talent and hard work on your part
attract opportunity as August ends. The
loving devotion of cherished animal
companions contributes to your overall happiness during September. The
autumnal equinox favors a pet blessing,
perhaps to welcome a new familiar.

October's transits will affect your
sector of mysteries and spiritual awakening. New information may surface to offer insight into a puzzle by
mid-month. Business associates will
feel the need to discuss finances as
All Hallows nears.

November 3 – 20 influences in your
9th house will put you in the mood
to explore and wander. Near the New
Moon in Scorpio on November 11,
you would enjoy cultivating a friendship with an acquaintance from another
land. Exotic cuisine and imports will be
appealing. A workshop or class might
interest you. Late November through
December your Sun is aspected by
transits in your 10th house. Ambition
and motivation soar. You'll strive for

recognition, prestige and success. Patiently perfecting your skills and expertise will assure achievement.

December 6 – 30 a harmonious Venus aspect promises some wonderful social invitations. Loving friends offer encouragement. Finances improve at the winter solstice. Light bayberry candles for prosperity. Place a tiny, potted evergreen tree on your altar. Eventually you could transplant it outdoors to grow into a towering symbol of your ideals and aspirations.

In January, Jupiter and Mercury turn retrograde. Your 7th and 11th houses, ruling partnerships and your circle of friends, respectively, will be affected. Examine previous situations regarding associates to reveal what will happen next. An important reunion brings a reminder that "there is no better mirror than an old friend." At Candlemas light two white votives. Dedicate one to the future and the other to honor the past.

Throughout February until March 5 Mars favorably aspects your Sun. Your energy level will be exceptional. Spiritual pursuits and academic studies enrich your life. Travel, especially near or over the water, would be rewarding. The Full Moon on February 22 offers insight regarding relationships. The Pisces eclipse on March 8 augurs exciting personal events. Dreams near your birthday foreshadow the specifics. Winter's final week finds transits of the Sun, Mercury, Venus and Neptune in your 1st house. This favors making important choices. Your communication skills will impress others with poetic eloquence.

HEALTH

The Sun rules your health sector. Invoke the solar energy at solstices and equinoxes to facilitate wellness throughout the year. Sunbathing, in moderation, is beneficial. It has an antiseptic effect on your body. Add a foot massage, as your birth sign rules the feet.

LOVE

Your vulnerability to criticism often casts shadows upon promising romances. The hypersensitive, Moon-ruled sign of Cancer oversees your love sector. Talk through hurtful situations with your partner then release any resentment, restoring loving kindness. Cosmic connections with Venus promise romantic bliss May 8 – June 5, December 6 – 30, and March 8 – 19.

SPIRITUALITY

With constant motion, moments glide, Behold! Running life's rolling tide! None stem by art or stop by pow'r, The flowing ocean or fleeting hour.
                                        – Minstrel, 1827

The riddle describes the Fish adrift in life's ocean on a soulful journey that's fathomed only by the divine. Nurture faith to discover spiritual awakening.

FINANCE

Eclipses on April 4 and September 27 impact your investments and earnings. A hobby may become a profit-making venture. Observe how changes in the economy affect your personal finances. Success arrives this year through recognizing current business trends. Update your skill set.

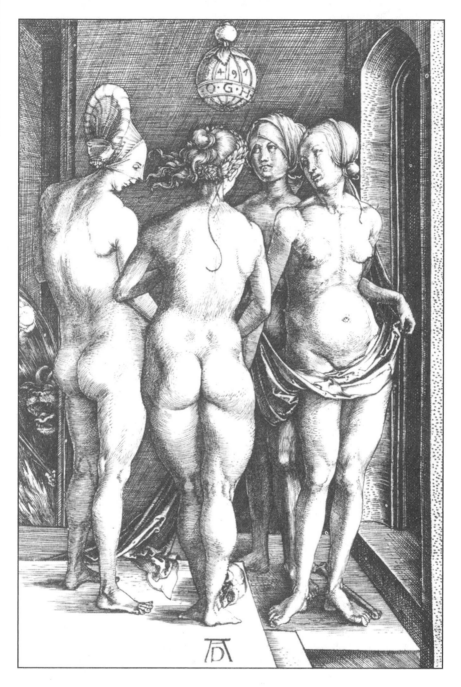

The Four Witches, Albrecht Dürer, 1497

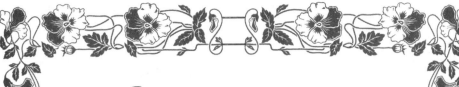

Sites of Awe

Verona, Italy – city of Shakespearian love

AS THE STORY GOES, or, as I have been told and come to believe, it was here in Verona that Juliet Capulet stood on her balcony, as Romeo Montague stood below, and the famous lines of love from William Shakespeare's *Romeo and Juliet* were spoken.

Act 2, scene 2 begins

But soft! What light through yonder window breaks?

It is the east, and Juliet is the sun.

Arise, fair sun, and kill the envious moon,

Who is already sick and pale with grief,

I am excited to be here in Verona, Italy. Last year I saw *Letters to Juliet*, the 2010 film starring one of my favorite actresses, Vanessa Redgrave. It is a love story like no other, based on archetypal love, just as Shakespeare had intended, when he wrote *Romeo and Juliet* in the late 16th century.

Real magic

Anyone who has ever been struck by Eros' arrow or felt the gentle touch of Aphrodite cannot help but get sweaty palms and feel butterflies in their stomach, as I do now, because I am turning down the street in Verona where I will find Juliet's balcony. Well, they say it isn't the real balcony of Juliet, because Juliet was a fictional character, invented by William Shakespeare. But I've read *Romeo and Juliet* and seen several versions of it and Juliet is more real to me than my neighbor's daughter, whose name I don't even remember. And that is good enough for me. Magic isn't based on what the populace believes is real, but rather what the magician believes is real, and I am coming here to do real magic.

The streets are crowded, but as I walk closer to what I think is the entrance to the balcony garden, I see more and more people. This must be the place — I'm getting very excited. Here I see what should be the stone tunnel that leads to the garden, like it did in the movie, but the walls are not stone. Someone has covered the stone wall with wood, probably to protect the mortar that holds the stones together. I imagine that following the movie last year, many visitors came here to pick and poke at the mortar, so they could, as tradition has it, insert their wishes and letters of love into the wall. The tunnel is crowded, but cooler than the street behind me. Numerous people are pushing their way inward and fighting their way past the people who are coming out. Seems to me there could be a better system here and a bit more harmony in place for a site surrounded in romance.

The passion that is love

Once inside, I see that it is not actually a garden, but a courtyard with trees and plants along the perimeter. On the far side is a bronze image of a woman; people are standing beside her, having their pictures taken – not what I am here for. There on the right is the balcony, not far above the ground level. To the left is a gift shop.

I'm backing up against the wall, now closing my eyes, using an exercise I learned many years ago: I tune out the voices and attempt to feel the energy of where I am. I am in awe of the fundamental emotion that I am feeling. Overwhelming waves of love, interspersed with friendship, compassion, empathy, tenderness, caring, and humility. This is not entirely what I expected. But, on second thought, I guess all of these feelings have something to do with the passion that is love. This is an experience that I will never forget – a treasure trove of emotion that I would like to save in a bottle for the rest of my life.

Pebble of power

Now that I am here, what should I do? I know! The first thing I need to do is to pick up a pebble. With all the tourists

here, searching around for a pebble that I know must have been here for a long time is not easy, but when traveling, it is always a good idea to look for spell components that are rare. What better for a love charm than to have a pebble from Juliet's courtyard?

On the opposite side of the courtyard there looks to be an old tree. As I walk over to it, I notice that the ground in which it is planted has loose and dry soil. Okay, I'll put my backpack on the ground in front of it and pretend to be fishing through it for something, but, really, I'll dig up a pebble that must have been here for many years. Found one! In the backpack it goes. What should I leave in exchange? I know, I'm going to write a letter of love of my own.

Letters and padlocks

A brief few sentences later, I am done. Tucking it under a loose root of the tree, I stand up, brush my hands off, and pretend that I am just like every other visitor. Many of the people here are buying padlocks in the gift shop. They write their name on it and the name of their intended love and then secure the lock to a large iron grate in the courtyard. It is covered with locks. A nice idea, but attaching a wish of love to a piece of iron is contrary to my magical training. I like the letter idea much better; it is "softer."

I've done everything I came here for and I've experienced the place that I have thought about for some time. Now, satisfied, it is time to leave. Walking out through the crowded tunnel of people, I take one last look back at the balcony and, to the left, at the tree between the gift shop and the wall of locks. I am happy to have a pebble in my backpack, but more happy to have left a note to my beloved at the roots of an old tree.

– ARMAND TABER

Find photos at
www.TheWitchesAlmanac.com/
MagicalSites.

From a Witch's Mailbox

Familiars

Do you think it's possible to have more than one familiar?

– Jennifer S.
Facebook

Most Witches believe there is a web of connectivity between all things. Embracing this belief promotes extraordinary bonds with living creatures. Given that, some witches believe that all pets are familiars. The emotional/spiritual/magical bond between witch and familiar is strong and deep. It is reciprocal, and like all significant relationships it requires time, attention and care. Caution should be taken against diluting the strength and quality of such special relationships by cultivating more than one can properly tend.

Imagery

Traditionally, I have built images in the candle's flame and sent them up to the heavens to bring about my intent in the universe's time. Does anyone else throw imagery with energy to bring about their desired ends?

– Corinne S
Facebook

Often referred to as creative visualization in secular settings, this technique is widely employed by athletes to enhance performance and achieve victory. Some simply call it the power of imagination.

Building and maintaining mental imagery is an exercise common to many spiritual practices. In terms of magic, projecting a desired outcome with focussed intent is one of the most effective paths to manifestation. It is indeed a powerful tool, but don't be deceived by its apparent simplicity. Precision and detail are the critical ingredients required to avoid creating unforeseen or unwanted related consequences. Focus is vital and requires practice to maintain. With appropriate training, practice and discipline, the results can be both predictable and astounding.

Sage

I'd like to know how the use of sage crossed over into witchcraft.?

– Susan A.
Facebook

Sage, Common Sage, or Salvia officinalis *has been viewed as a sacred herb with magical properties throughout the ages and across many cultures. Childless couples employed sage to increase fertility both in Egypt and ancient Rome. Sage is featured repeatedly in European folklore: fresh leaves were used in love oracles; dried leaves were burned to erase negativity. Sage was commonly planted in graveyards due to its power to ease grief and sprigs were brushed over persons suffering from nightmares to dispel these bad dreams. Long associated with strength, vitality and longevity, Sage conveyed good health or strength in Floriography. For instructions on creating a sage bath that will lift the spirits and increase vitality, see our* Herbal Notes *article in the 1993 — 1994 issue.*

Salvia apiana, commonly known as White Sage or Bee Sage is native to the southwestern United States; rarely found beyond the borders of California. Widely used by Native Americans on the Pacific coast, it is an important ceremonial plant used primarily for cleansing and purification. Many non-Natives have "borrowed" white sage and the ritual technique of smudging to clear away negative energy and/or create sacred space. However, it should be noted that traditional smudging is a sacred ritual, with prescribed steps, carried out in a sacred way.

Names

What are thoughts on having and using a magical name? How does one choose?

– Christi D.
Facebook

The adoption of magical names is common. How and why is often determined by cultural context; e.g., in some traditions a name is either given or earned, while in others a name is chosen by the individual with little or no guidance. Two common premises for chosen names are affinity or aspiration. In most magical traditions, to name something is to give it power or bring it to life. In that context, care should be taken to choose a name representing qualities that one desires to manifest in oneself.

Origins

What are some of the legends of origin for witches?

– Jonathan S.
Facebook

Interesting topic, but a bit thorny in the world of witchcraft. Keep in mind that most would say being a witch involves access to oath-bound material which cannot be shared outside the coven or tradition. Most origin legends would fall squarely in that category. And then there's the problem of who's qualified to say who is a witch. For some an origin legend is a family history, while for others it's an accepted mythology. However, one of the most well-known origin legends was published by the renowned folklorist, Charles G. Leland in 1899; a book titled Aradia, Gospel of the Witches. *We published a special edition that preserves the original text and includes commentary from some of the most respective modern voices in the Craft. Go to http://thewitchesalmanac.com/aradia.html and get your copy today.*

Let us hear from you, too

We love to hear from our readers. Letters should be sent with the writer's name (or just first name or initials), address, daytime phone number and e-mail address, if available. Published material may be edited for clarity or length. All letters and e-mails will become the property of The Witches' Almanac Ltd. *and will not be returned. We regret that due to the volume of correspondence we cannot reply to all communications.*

The Witches' Almanac, Ltd.
P.O. Box 1292
Newport, RI 02840-9998
info@TheWitchesAlmanac.com
www.TheWitchesAlmanac.com

Reviews

Alchemy Works
http://www.alchemy-works.com

THERE ARE a plethora of sites on the Web offering magical commodities ranging from typical occult ware to the rare find. Harold Roth's Alchemy Works falls into the latter category, offering oils, incenses, and resins crafted for the discerning witch with a discriminating magical palette. Of special note is their Galangal Oil, which could be considered by far the best available on the Web today!

With an easy and unassuming interface, shopping for the perfect oil has never been easier than at Alchemy Works. That being said, this site is not just for the consumer, it is also for the student. Along with the each item for sale is a tidbit about the item. For example, the shopper for oils is not simply provided a list of items for sale, the oils page also informs as to their planetary attribution. Clicking on the oil name brings you to a page with the pricing. Choosing the planetary attribution brings you to a page containing a table rich in content regarding the planet. You will find similar links on the seeds and herbs pages.

Alchemy Works also provides a number of stand-alone educational pages. For instance, the page entitled

Making a Flower Essence provides one of the most concise guides to making flower essences this author has ever come across. Be sure to check the *Herbal Codes* page that provides a list of herbs with their code names, allowing us to unravel the secret language of grimoires. Armed with knowledge from this page, when you come across a recipe calling for Hare's Beard, rather than chasing a poor little bunny with a razor and shaving cream, you will simply go out and procure the proper herb, Great Mullein.

Mystical Origins of the Tarot: From Ancient Roots to Modern Usage
ISBN-13: 978-0-89281-190-8
Destiny Books
Price: $19.95

PAUL HUSON has given us a rich tome on the tarot that presumes nothing and casts a wide net of investigation. In a grand departure from The Devil's Picturebook, his earlier work on the speculative tarot, here Huson presents a more scholarly piece.

Driving this work are the three questions that Huson poses in his preface:
• What was the origin of the suit card symbols and what did they stand for?

- What was the source of the trumps and what was their original import?
- When and why did people begin using the cards for divination — that is, as a means of acquiring spiritual guidance or discovering hidden information?

Huson meticulously guides us through these questions, while infusing them with a sound understanding of the medieval. Many authors begin their journey through the tarot with the Major Arcana. Huson however, begins his journey with the Minor Arcana, exploring the origins of the suits. In a radical departure from other authors, Huson examines the implications of the social strata of medieval society progressing backward to Persia. Huson explores a broad range of opinions and theories regarding the suits without falling into the trap of scholastic rigor mortis.

What follows is a rare take on the Major Arcana and their possible reflective state of Medieval Theatre. Huson very neatly puts forth some very specific references to the trump cards and their connection to the popular entertainment of the era in which they developed. Huson's examination of the origins of the divinatory use of tarot is poignant. He delves into the possible origins in a simple French method; he follows that to the era of the Golden Dawn.

The meat of *Mystical Origins of the Tarot* is in the balance of the book. Huson journeys us through the tarot starting with the Trumps (Major Arcana), Court Cards of the Minor Arcana, and finally to the numbered cards of the Minor Arcana. He treats us to a goodly amount of black and white art depicting images from decks that have long since disappeared from everyday use. Huson provides alternate names of each of the cards, an examination of background lore, original cartomantic interpretation, and finally suggested interpretations.

Huson brings his treatise to a conclusion with an in-depth examination of reading the tarot, speaking to his method of developing interpretive narrative. Few authors take the time to push the apprentice reader to develop such skill. He closes his book with appendices exploring historical decks and where to see them, as well as sources for modern decks.

Lindsay Adler
Spirals of Love
http://www.lindsayadler.com

LINDSAY ADLER is a uniquely talented American Celtic vocal artist whose compositions and performance range from plaintive ethereal voice to jubilant story teller. Her recent offering *Spirals of Love* is a truly fine showcase for her broad vocal range and style. Ms. Adler has taken the Celtic art of storytelling to new heights, giving you not only the narrative but painting rich scenes that color the mind.

Opening with *Seven Swans*, we are immediately whisked away in the bath of love with the metaphor of swans to guide us through the wonder of it all. In a few instances, Ms. Adler forgoes the voice, letting our minds tells the story as her fingers tumble over her guitar strings with exuberance and finesse. Such is the case also with *Triple Spiral Waltz*, during which this author danced his heart away with past loves.

Ms. Adler defines herself on her website as "a multi-instrumentalist, vocalist and composer who seamlessly bridges the gap between ancient and modern folk music." Indeed she is and does, while allowing the listener to journey the byways with her.

Krampus!
Image Comics Inc.
https://imagecomics.com/comics/releases/krampus-1

KRAMPUS! is a tongue-in-cheek adaptation of what might have happened to the Krampus in modern times. Don't expect esoteric lore or mystical musings in this amusing set. It's strictly comic book-style storytelling and imagination run wild like a kid in a candy store. But I liked it!

In its own way, this offering proves that old myths die hard, that each generation of popular culture recycles the dreams and nightmares of the past and dresses them up to look more familiar, as well as fit in with current style. It's good clean fun with sardonic undertones and just a splash of blasphemy. With the story by Brian Joines and art by Dean Kotz, *Krampus!* can be found on eBay or your local comics store for back issues. Digital editions can also be purchased directly from the publisher.

The Museum of Witchcraft

Image by John Hooper Hoopix / Museum of Witchcraft ©2014

OUR GOOD FRIENDS at the Museum of Witchcraft have announced some changes. On April 1st, 2014, the museum opened under new management, with Peter and Judith Hewitt taking over the day-to-day management, overseen by the Museum of British Folklore. Graham King, the previous manager, is helping with the handover process and preparations for the new season. To see their press release check out the link at http://TheWitchesAlmanac.com/MagicalSites/.

In case you did not know, the Museum of Witchcraft is located in Boscastle, Cornwall, England. It houses one of the world's largest collections of witchcraft-related artifacts. The museum has been located in Boscastle for fifty years and is amongst Cornwall's most popular museums.

a Circle Sanctuary publication

Circle Magazine

Celebrating Nature, Spirit, and Magic

Inspiring and connecting Pagans for over 35 years!

CIRCLE Magazine is a quarterly publication featuring articles, artwork, poetry, rituals and inspiration by and for the Pagan and Nature Spirituality community.

Subscribe at www.circlesanctuary.org/circle

The products and services offered above are paid advertisements.

The Witchcraft of Dame Darrel of York

Charles Godfrey Leland

Introduction by Robert Mathiesen

The Witches' Almanac presents:

• *A previously unpublished work by folklorist Charles Godfrey Leland.*

• *Published in full color facsimile with a text transcript.*

• *Forward by Prof. Robert Mathiesen.*

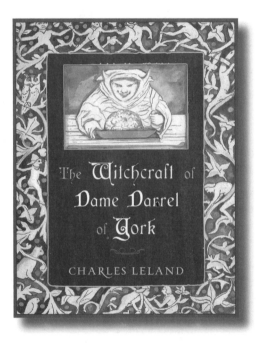

This beautifully reproduced facsimile of the illuminated manuscript will shed light on an ancient tradition as well as provide the basis for a modern practice. It will be treasured by those practicing Pagans, scholars, and all those fascinated by the legend and lore of England.

Standard hardcover edition ($65.00).
Deluxe numbered edition with slipcase ($85.00).
Exclusive full leather bound, numbered and slip cased edition ($145.00).

For further information visit http://TheWitchesAlmanac.com/damedarrel.html

ARADIA
GOSPEL OF THE WITCHES
Charles Godfrey Leland

ARADIA IS THE FIRST work in English in which witchcraft is portrayed as an underground old religion, surviving in secret from ancient pagan times.

• Used as a core text by many modern neo-pagans.

• Foundation material containing traditional witchcraft practices

• This special edition features appreciations by such authors and luminaries as Paul Huson, Raven Grimassi, Judika Illes, Michael Howard, Christopher Penczak, Myth Woodling, Christina Oakley Harrington, Patricia Della-Piana, Jimahl di Fiosa and Donald Weiser. A beautiful and compelling work, this edition has brought the format up to date, while keeping the text unchanged. 172 pages $16.95

⋇ Newly expanded classics! ⋇

The ABC of Magic Charms
Elizabeth Pepper

SINCE THE DAWN of mankind, an obscure instinct in the human spirit has sought protection from mysterious forces beyond mortal control. Human beings sought benefaction in the three realms that share Earth with us — animal, mineral, vegetable. All three, humanity discovered, contain mysterious properties discovered over millennia through occult divination. An enlarged edition of *Magic Charms from A to Z*, compiled by the staff of *The Witches' Almanac*. $12.95

The Little Book of Magical Creatures
Elizabeth Pepper and Barbara Stacy
A loving tribute to the animal kingdom

AN UPDATE of the classic *Magical Creatures*, featuring Animals Tame, Animals Wild, Animals Fabulous – plus an added section of enchanting animal myths from other times, other places. *A must for all animal lovers.* $12.95

♣ a lady shape-shifts into a white doe ♣ two bears soar skyward
♣ Brian Boru rides a wild horse ♣ a wolf growls dire prophecy

ANCIENT ROMAN HOLIDAYS

The glory that was Rome awaits you in Barbara Stacy's classic presentation of a festive year in pagan times. Here are the gods and goddesses as the Romans conceived them, accompanied by the annual rites performed in their worship. Scholarly, light-hearted – a rare combination.

CELTIC TREE MAGIC

Robert Graves in *The White Goddess* writes of the significance of trees in the old Celtic lore. *Celtic Tree Magic* is an investigation of the sacred trees in the remarkable Beth-Luis-Nion alphabet; their role in folklore, poetry, and mysticism.

MOON LORE

As both the largest and the brightest object in the night sky, and the only one to appear in phases, the Moon has been a rich source of myth for as long as there have been mythmakers.

MAGIC SPELLS AND INCANTATIONS

Words have magic power. Their sound, spoken or sung, has ever been a part of mystic ritual. From ancient Egypt to the present, those who practice the art of enchantment have drawn inspiration from a treasury of thoughts and themes passed down through the ages.

LOVE FEASTS

Creating meals to share with the one you love can be a sacred ceremony in itself. With the witch in mind, culinary adept Christine Fox offers magical menus and recipes for every month in the year.

RANDOM RECOLLECTIONS II, III, IV

Pages culled from the original (no longer available) issues of *The Witches' Almanac*, published annually throughout the 1970's, are now available in a series of tasteful booklets. A treasure for those who missed us the first time around; keepsakes for those who remember.

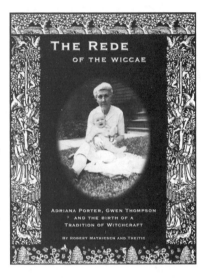
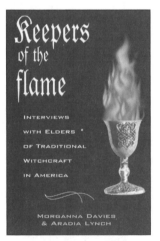

Order Form

Each timeless edition of *The Witches' Almanac* is unique.
Limited numbers of previous years' editions are available.

Item	Price	Qty.	Total
2015-2016 The Witches' Almanac	$12.95		
2014-2015 The Witches' Almanac	$12.95		
2013-2014 The Witches' Almanac	$11.95		
2012-2013 The Witches' Almanac	$11.95		
2011-2012 The Witches' Almanac	$11.95		
2010-2011 The Witches' Almanac	$11.95		
2009-2010 The Witches' Almanac	$11.95		
2008-2009 The Witches' Almanac	$10.95		
2007-2008 The Witches' Almanac	$9.95		
2006-2007 The Witches' Almanac	$8.95		
2005-2006 The Witches' Almanac	$8.95		
2004-2005 The Witches' Almanac	$8.95		
2003-2004 The Witches' Almanac	$8.95		
2002-2003 The Witches' Almanac	$7.95		
2001-2002 The Witches' Almanac	$7.95		
2000-2001 The Witches' Almanac	$7.95		
1999-2000 The Witches' Almanac	$7.95		
1998-1999 The Witches' Almanac	$6.95		
1997-1998 The Witches' Almanac	$6.95		
1996-1997 The Witches' Almanac	$6.95		
1995-1996 The Witches' Almanac	$6.95		
1994-1995 The Witches' Almanac	$5.95		
1993-1994 The Witches' Almanac	$5.95		
The Witchcraft of Dame Darrel of York, clothbound	$65.00		
Aradia or The Gospel of the Witches	$16.95		
The Horned Shepherd	$16.95		
The ABC of Magic Charms	$12.95		
The Little Book of Magical Creatures	$12.95		
Greek Gods in Love	$15.95		
Witches All	$13.95		
Ancient Roman Holidays	$6.95		
Celtic Tree Magic	$7.95		
Love Charms	$6.95		
Love Feasts	$6.95		
Magic Charms from A to Z	$12.95		
Magical Creatures	$12.95		
Magic Spells and Incantations	$12.95		
Moon Lore	$7.95		
Random Recollections II, III or IV (circle your choices)	$3.95		
SALE 20 back issues with free book bag and free shipping	$100.00		
The Rede of the Wiccae	$22.95		
Keepers of the Flame	$20.95		
Subtotal			
Tax (7% sales tax for RI customers)			
Shipping & Handling *(See shipping rates section)*			
TOTAL			

BRACELETS			
Item	Price	Qty.	Total
Agate, Green	$5.95		
Agate, Moss	$5.95		
Agate, Natural	$5.95		
Agate, Red	$5.95		
Amethyst	$5.95		
Aventurine	$5.95		
Fluorite	$5.95		
Jade, African	$5.95		
Jade, White	$5.95		
Jasper, Picture	$5.95		
Jasper, Red	$5.95		
Lapis Lazuli	$5.95		
Malachite	$5.95		
Moonstone	$5.95		
Obsidian	$5.95		
Onyx, Black	$5.95		
Opal	$5.95		
Quartz Crystal	$5.95		
Quartz, Rose	$5.95		
Rhodonite	$5.95		
Sodalite	$5.95		
Tigereye	$5.95		
Turquoise	$5.95		
Unakite	$5.95		
Subtotal			
Tax (7% for RI customers)			
Shipping & Handling (See shipping rates section)			
TOTAL			

MISCELLANY			
Item	Price	Qty.	Total
Pouch	$3.95		
Matches: *10 small individual boxes*	$5.00		
Matches: *1 large box of 50 individual boxes*	$20.00		
Natural/Black Book Bag	$17.95		
Red/Black Book Bag	$17.95		
Hooded Sweatshirt, Blk	$30.00		
Hooded Sweatshirt, Red	$30.00		
L-Sleeve T, Black	$20.00		
L-Sleeve T, Red	$20.00		
S-Sleeve T, Black/W	$15.00		
S-Sleeve T, Black/R	$15.00		
S-Sleeve T, Dk H/R	$15.00		
S-Sleeve T, Dk H/W	$15.00		
S-Sleeve T, Red/B	$15.00		
S-Sleeve T, Ash/R	$15.00		
S-Sleeve T, Purple/W	$15.00		
Postcards – set of 12	$3.00		
Bookmarks – set of 12	$1.00		
Magnets – set of 3	$1.50		
Promo Pack	$7.00		
Subtotal			
Tax (7% sales tax for RI customers)			
Shipping & Handling (See shipping rates section)			
TOTAL			

SHIPPING & HANDLING CHARGES

BOOKS: One book, add $4.00. Each additional book add $1.50

POUCH: One pouch, $2.00. Each additional pouch add $1.50

MATCHES: Ten individual boxes, add $2.50.
One large box of fifty, add $6.00. Each additional large box add $3.50.

BOOKBAGS: $4.00 per bookbag.

BRACELETS: $2.00 per bracelet.

Send a check or money order payable in U. S. funds or credit card details to:

The Witches' Almanac, Ltd., PO Box 1292, Newport, RI 02840-9998

(401) 847-3388 (phone) • (888) 897-3388 (fax)
Email: info@TheWitchesAlmanac.com • www.TheWitchesAlmanac.com